QUICK & EASY LOW-SUGAR RECIPES

LOSE WEIGHT · BOOST ENERGY · FIGHT FATIGUE

NICOLA GRAIMES

WATKINS PUBLISHING

LONDON

This edition published in the UK in 2010 by
Watkins Publishing, Sixth Floor, Castle House,
75–76 Wells Street, London W1T 3QH

1 3 5 7 9 10 8 6 4 2

Designed and typeset by Jerry Goldie Graphic Design

Printed and bound in Great Britain

British Library Cataloguing-in-Publication data available

ISBN: 978-1-906787-61-5

www.watkinspublishing.co.uk

Publisher's Note: While every care has been taken in compiling the recipes for this book, Watkins Publishers, or any other persons who have been involved in working on this publication, cannot accept responsibility for any errors or omissions, inadvertent or not, that may be found in the recipes or text, nor for any problems that may arise as a result of preparing one of these recipes. If you are pregnant or breastfeeding or have any special dietary requirements or medical conditions, it is advisable to consult a medical professional before following any of the recipes contained in this book. Ill or elderly people, babies, young children and women who are pregnant or breastfeeding should avoid any recipes containing uncooked egg whites.

Contents

Food warning symbols   vi

About this book   1

Basic Low-Sugar Recipes   17

Breakfasts & Brunches   25

Light Meals & Snacks   57

Dinners   99

Desserts   139

Cakes, Bakes & Breads   191

Menu Plans   228

Index   232

FOOD WARNING SYMBOLS

If you or a member of your family is vegetarian or has an allergy to or intolerance of nuts, eggs, seeds, gluten, wheat or dairy products, you will find these symbols, which accompany each recipe, invaluable. Any added sugar is also identified.

- Ⓥ   vegetarian
- ⓪   contains nuts
- ⓞ   contains eggs
- ⓢ   contains seeds
- Ⓖ   contains gluten
- Ⓦ   contains wheat
- Ⓓ   contains dairy
- Ⓢ   contains added sugar

In addition, the menu plans on pages 228–31 give ideas for a week's worth of meals for wheat- and gluten-free, vegetarian, vegan and nut-free diets.

Notes on the recipes

Please note that metric and imperial measurements are given for the recipes. Follow one set of measures only, not a mixture, as they are not interchangeable.

- 1 tsp = 5ml   1 tbsp = 15ml   1 cup = 250ml

Unless otherwise stated:
- Use medium/large eggs
- Use medium fruit and vegetables
- Use fresh herbs

ABOUT THIS BOOK

The aim of this book is to inspire you to cook recipes that are low in sugar and full of nutritious, wholesome ingredients. The recipes will suit the whole family or can be adjusted to serve just one or two people. They are simple and quick to prepare. Many will keep for a few days in the refrigerator, whilst others can be frozen for future use, allowing you to plan ahead and take the hassle out of mealtimes. Choose from an inspiring range of world flavours from different cuisines as well as low-sugar versions of family favourites.

The following collection of recipes shows that eating low-sugar foods doesn't mean you're condemned to a dull diet. The good news is that there are numerous naturally sweet foods and alternative flavourings that will help you to create nutritious and delicious breakfasts, meals, snacks and even cakes and desserts. Importantly, there's no need to resort to artificial sweeteners, which have well-documented adverse health effects if consumed in large quantities.

Quick & Easy Low-Sugar Recipes makes an important distinction between '**added**' refined sugars and sugars found '**naturally**' in fruit, vegetables and wholegrain carbohydrates. **Added** sugars are refined sugars found predominantly in processed foods and as everyday sugar (sucrose). These are often referred to as calorie-rich and nutritionally poor, since they contain little in the way of nutritional value. By contrast, sugars found **naturally** in fruit (fructose) play a key part in the recipes in this book. Along with providing sweetness, fruit is also a good source of beneficial vitamins, minerals, phytochemicals and fibre.

Natural sweeteners are used in some of the recipes – particularly in the chapters on desserts, cakes and biscuits. These are mainly fructose, xylitol and agave syrup, which, along with adding a desired sweetness, also have some health benefits (see Sugar Alternatives, page 8). Nevertheless, as with any type of sugar, they should be eaten on an occasional basis and in moderate amounts.

There are many beneficial reasons to choose low-sugar foods or indeed opt for the wider parameters of a low-sugar diet: from the prevention of dental caries and wrinkles to weight loss and steady energy levels. However, there's more to a low-sugar diet than simply cutting down on sugary foods, or cutting them out altogether. Low-sugar diets also involve reducing your intake of refined carbohydrates, including white bread, white rice and processed foods. These foods have a similar negative affect on blood-sugar levels as refined sugar. Get into the habit of reading food labels too (see Read the Label, page 13), as many processed foods contain hidden added sugars.

All the recipes have been created to suit people with diabetes and to meet their dietary requirements. This means that they are low in not only sugar but also salt and saturated fat, and high in fibre.

When following a low-sugar diet, try to avoid eating a dessert, cake or biscuit every day, even if sweetened naturally. These foods are also frequently high in fat and will eventually lead to weight gain if eaten to excess. The key is to re-train your palate to enjoy foods with lower levels of sugar. Adjust your palate gradually, and try experimenting with different flavourings such as herbs and spices – cinnamon, nutmeg and vanilla add a wonderful depth of flavour and aroma to desserts and cakes.

WHAT IS SUGAR?

Sugar (sucrose) is a refined or simple carbohydrate that is sweet-tasting and comes in numerous different forms, many of which derive from sugar cane or sugar beet. Generally, sugars have names that end in 'ose", such as sucrose, dextrose, maltose, galactose, lactose (found in milk) and fructose (found in fruit).

Yet there are many others that you need to be aware of when

cutting down on sugar (see Read the Label, page 13). the same caloric value of other carbohydrates: 4 calories per gram. One teaspoon of sugar contains 15 calories.

UNDERSTANDING CARBOHYDRATES

Reducing your intake of added sugars is only part of the story, since it's also relevant to understand more about carbohydrates and how they work in the body if looking to follow a low-sugar diet.

Despite being the focus of much controversy, with some diets advocating severely restricting carbohydrate intake, there is no denying the fact that this food group plays an essential part of our diet and is our main source of energy. Yet it's all about eating the right sort of carbs and in reasonable amounts.

There are two types of carbohydrate – sugar and starches – both of which are available in their natural and processed form:
• natural sugar (fructose) found in fruit and vegetables
• refined sugars or simple sugars such as white and brown sugar (sucrose)
• unrefined starches, also known as complex carbohydrates, found in wholegrain pasta, brown rice, wholegrain cereals, lentils, pulses and root vegetables
• refined starches found in white pasta, white flour, white bread, white rice and processed sugary breakfast cereals

Ideally, our diets should be based on fruits, vegetables and unrefined starches ("good' carbs), as these provide a range of beneficial nutrients and fibre. By contrast, refined sugars and starches have had much of their value removed during processing.

What's more, sugary refined foods are said to cause rapid changes in blood-sugar levels in our bodies, leading to highs and subsequent lows. Peaks and troughs in blood-sugar levels adversely affect energy levels and can lead to mood swings, irritability and hunger pangs. The fibre content of unrefined carbs, on the other hand, encourages the slow release of sugars (glucose) into the blood, which then have a more stabilizing affect on energy levels.

SUGAR AND HEALTH

It is widely acknowledged that we eat far too much sugar, and dietary experts worldwide believe that this could have serious repercussions on our health. A diet high in sugar has been linked to dental decay, obesity, hyperactivity, depression, chronic fatigue and mood swings. Diabetics and those suffering with heart problems, hyperglycaemia and syndrome X are also encouraged to curb their sugar intake.

A report by the World Health Organisation (WHO) in 2006 recommends that 'added' sugars should make up no more than 10 per cent of daily calorie intake.

Average daily carbohydrate/sugar requirement for adults:
Women:
Cals/day 1,900   Total carbs/day 255g/9oz   Added sugar/day 50g/2oz

Men:
Cals/day 2,550   Total carbs/day 340g/12oz   Added sugar/day 68g/2½oz

This means that women should limit their daily consumption of added sugars to around 50g/1¾oz (10 teaspoons) and men to around 70g/2½oz (14 teaspoons). Yet the typical diet of many people in Western countries is double this amount on a daily basis. To put this into perspective, eat three chocolate biscuits (30g/1oz sugar) and drink two cups of coffee, each sweetened with 2 teaspoons (10g/¼oz) of sugar, and you reach the maximum recommended level, whilst a can of cola has around 36g/1¼oz sugar.

Evidence suggests that children are particularly susceptible to the adverse side affects of a high-sugar diet, namely hyperactivity, behavioural difficulties, mood swings, fatigue and obesity, and studies reveal that incidences of these disorders are on the increase. A recent UK government report shows that almost one in 10 children starting primary school is obese, and unfortunately this problem is not restricted to any one country. Poor diet can also influence a child's health later in life, increasing the risk of diabetes, cancer and heart disease.

A diet low in sugar is usually prescribed for people with hypoglycaemia and hyperglycaemia. Hypoglycaemia is a medical condition whereby the pancreas releases too much insulin as a result of a rapid rise in blood sugar, which results in an abnormally low blood-sugar level. Conversely, hyperglycaemia, or high blood sugar, is a condition in which an excessive amount of glucose circulates in the bloodstream. Severe hyperglycaemia can occur if you eat a very sugary food, or if your body has not produced enough insulin.

The hormone insulin plays a major role in converting sugars into energy in the body, but if you are overweight, take little exercise and eat too many sugary and processed foods, you may become insulin resistant. This means that insulin levels remain too high and in turn contribute to excess fat in the body. Signs of insulin resistance, or syndrome X, include cravings for carbs, mood swings, tiredness and feeling 'fuggy".

However, everyone benefits from a low-sugar diet because with this diet energy is stored and used more efficiently by the body. When sugar intake is moderated, the body's energy levels are constant. Controlling sugar intake also helps to regulate your appetite and keep food cravings at bay.

SUGAR CRAVINGS

Many of us regularly experience sugar cravings and they often coincide with a lull in energy levels, particularly mid-afternoon. An increased desire for something sweet may be attributed to a drop in blood-sugar levels, causing the body to compensate by desiring an instant fix. The reason why this often occurs in the afternoon is that the body may have experienced a temporary high in blood sugar after lunch, especially after eating something like a sandwich or other refined carbohydrate food.

One way to avoid such cravings is to work at keeping blood-sugar levels steady by eating regular meals/snacks based on foods such as unrefined carbohydrates combined with protein foods. These foods produce a more sustained effect on blood-sugar levels, because they are broken down more slowly in the body and avoid undesirable peaks and troughs.

SUGAR AND THE HEART

In the past, there has been a focus on saturated fat being a major risk factor in heart disease, but recent research shows that carbo-hydrates, particularly high GI foods (see page 12), may play a greater role than was originally thought. The problem lies in the effect that sugary foods, as well as refined carbohydrates such as white bread, pasta and rice, have on blood-sugar levels. Research has found that these foods have an unsettling effect, and the more blood sugar rises after a meal, the greater the risk of developing cardiovascular disease in the long term. Even transient rises in blood sugar may be a risk factor.

Peaks in blood-sugar levels also encourage free radical damage, affect circulation and increase the likelihood of blood clots. This may go some way to explaining why diabetics have an increased risk of heart disease, as they generally have increased levels of blood sugar.

SUGAR AND DIABETES

The number of people diagnosed with diabetes has jumped more than 60 per cent in the UK in just 10 years, and newly released figures found that an increase in obesity was fuelling the soaring rates. In the six-year period 1997–2003, the number of new cases soared 74 per cent, and they rose 63 per cent across the entire decade. In addition, the number of cases of Type 1 diabetes, which usually develops in childhood, and Type 2 diabetes, which is linked to obesity, rose dramatically between 1996 and 2005. These findings suggest that the number of diabetes sufferers in the UK is increasing faster than in the US, where prevalence of the disease is one of the highest in the world.

Diet is the cornerstone of controlling diabetes, enabling you to keep blood-sugar levels within the desired range, lower blood pressure, avoid hyperglycaemia, reduce the risk of heart problems (see above) and control your weight. A strict dietary regime is not necessary if you have diabetes, nor do you have to cut out sugar or severely restrict carbohydrate intake; however, it is important to eat a healthy balanced diet that is low in sugar and saturated fat and high in fibre, and to cut your intake of high GI foods.

SUGAR AND AGEING

There is now evidence to suggest that sugar can have an adverse affect on the skin, causing wrinkles and accelerating the ageing process. To blame is a natural process known as glycation, whereby sugar, or more accurately glucose, in the bloodstream attaches to proteins to form harmful new molecules called 'advanced glycation end products' (or, rather appropriately, AGEs). Most vulnerable to damage are collagen and elastin, which are responsible for keeping the skin firm and elastic. Glycation increases with the more sugar you eat, but the following steps help to keep your sugar intake in check and in turn look after your skin.

- Cut your intake of added sugar to 10 per cent of calories (see page 4).
- Watch out for hidden sugars that can lurk in all manner of

processed foods (see pages 13–15).
- Increase your intake of antioxidant-rich foods such as fruit, vegetables, nuts and seeds, especially those rich in vitamins C and E as well as beta carotene (converted to vitamin A in the body). The glycation process damages antioxidants through the creation of harmful free radicals, but you can redress the balance through eating foods that are high in antioxidants.
- Vitamins B1 and B6 are known to be AGE inhibitors. These nutrients are found in fruit, vegetables, whole grains, eggs, meat, poultry, seafood, pulses and nuts.

SUGAR ALTERNATIVES

It would be a dull life without the occasional treat, so some recipes in this book call for natural added sugars in the form of fructose, xylitol or agave syrup. Each is largely interchangeable, but do not forget that just because the cakes, biscuits and desserts are lower in sugar than their regular counterparts, they should remain treats.

Fructose

Fructose is a fruit sugar found naturally in fruit and vegetables and also in a crystallized form for home cooking.
- It does not cause a rapid rise and subsequent large fall in blood-sugar levels, which means it has a low glycaemic load or glycaemic index.
- It can be used in the same way as ordinary sugar (sucrose) and is suitable for cooking and baking. When baking, reduce the oven temperature by 25°C/50°F/1 gas mark.
- It is up to one-third sweeter than ordinary sugar, so less is required to achieve the desired sweetness.
- There is evidence to suggest that small amounts of fructose aid the processing of glucose in the body.
- It does not trigger the production of insulin because it is

metabolized by the liver, so may offer benefits for diabetics.
- Note that a small amount of fructose is not harmful to health, but recent research has shown that consuming excessive amounts in one go seems to overwhelm the body's capacity to process it. Instead, the body produces fat from the fructose and releases it into the body in the form of triglycerides.

Xylitol

This is a naturally occurring substance that looks and tastes just like sugar. It is found in many plants and fruits, such as raspberries, plums and strawberries, and is even made in small amounts by the human body. The xylitol sold in a granular form is a processed sugar alcohol and is generally made from wood.
- It does not cause a rapid rise and subsequent fall in blood-sugar levels, which means it has a low glycaemic load or index.
- It has 40 per cent fewer calories than sugar and may reduce sugar cravings.
- It can be used in the same way as ordinary sugar (sucrose) and is suitable for cooking and baking. When baking, reduce the oven temperature by 25°C/50°F/1 gas mark.
- It has only 75 per cent of the available carbohydrates of sugar, making it a useful way to add sweetness to food and drinks without overloading on carbohydrates.
- It has a minimal impact on insulin and glucose levels; therefore xylitol has no requirement on insulin to be metabolized.
- It may help those with osteoporosis by improving bone density.
- It promotes healthy teeth and reduces plaque and dental decay.
- It may help to control *Candida albicans*, an overgrowth of yeast in the body.

Agave syrup or nectar

The agave plant has long been cultivated in Mexico, where it was considered sacred and believed to be able to purify the body and soul. Its fleshy leaves cover the pineapple-shaped heart of the plant, which contains a sweet sticky juice. The syrup is a good replacement for golden syrup, honey or maple syrup.

- It does not cause a rapid rise and subsequent large fall in blood-sugar levels, which means it has a low glycaemic load or glycaemic index.
- Unrefined agave nectar is a natural source of iron, calcium, potassium and magnesium, as well as vitamins A, C and E.
- It can be used in the same way as ordinary sugar (sucrose) and is suitable for cooking and baking. When baking, reduce the oven temperature by 25°C/50°F/1 gas mark.
- It is up to 25 per cent sweeter than ordinary sugar, so less is required to achieve the desired sweetness.
- It has a minimal impact on insulin and glucose levels.

HIGH-FRUCTOSE CORN SYRUP

At the forefront of recent negative publicity, high-fructose corn syrup (HFCS) has been blamed for the increasing incidence of obesity in the US. Made from cornstarch, HFCS is made up of two types of sugar, fructose and glucose, and has become the cornerstone of processed foods – both sweet and savoury. HFCS is cheaper than sugar, and, due to its chemical structure, it can prolong the shelf-life of products.

There is evidence to suggest that HFCS may circumvent the normal appetite-regulating hormones in the body, encouraging over-eating, which may go some way to explain why excessive consumption is linked with weight gain, especially around the abdomen.

Other research shows that excessive consumption may be linked with insulin resistance, possibly encouraging Type 2 diabetes.

SWITCHING TO A LOW-SUGAR DIET

- Aim to eat plenty of different types of fruit and vegetables a day. (In the UK, five portions are the target to reach, while in Australia it's six and in the US it's nine.) Eat proportionally more fresh or frozen than canned or juiced. Fresh produce is a rich source of vitamins, minerals and fibre, and is naturally filling, helping to curb cravings for processed sugary foods.
- If buying canned fruit, look for fruit in natural juice rather than in syrup.
- Replace high-sugar breakfast cereals with porridge, homemade muesli or wholegrain cereals with no added sugar.
- Although rich in vitamins, minerals and enzymes, juiced fruit and vegetables lose much of their fibre content, which means their natural sugars enter the bloodstream quickly, creating spikes and subsequent falls in blood-sugar levels. One glass a day is fine, though.
- Make your own dressings, marinades, sauces (sweet and savoury) and fruit compotes.
- Use fresh and dried fruit to add natural sweetness and moisture to cakes.
- Alongside fresh produce, 'good' carbs (see Understanding Carbohydrates, page 3) provide slow-release energy and will help to curb hunger pangs and the urge to snack.
- Eat three healthy meals a day to provide sustained amounts of energy: a combination of complex carbs, low-fat protein and a small amount of healthy fats is recommended, not forgetting plenty of fruit and veg.
- Drink alcohol in moderation, and avoid drinking it on an empty stomach – not only is it high in sugar but it can also adversely affect blood-sugar levels.
- Check food labels (see Read the Label, page 13) to avoid hidden sugars.

GLYCAEMIC INDEX AND GLYCAEMIC LOAD

The foundation of most low-carb diets, the glycaemic index (GI) is a way of working out how a food is likely to affect blood-sugar levels. All carbs have a ranking of 0 to 100. The lower a food's GI, the longer it takes to be digested and the smaller the rise in blood-sugar levels and insulin response. Foods with a high GI value have a more dramatic affect on blood-sugar levels, leading to yo-yoing energy levels, hunger pangs, mood swings and tiredness. There are some surprises in the GI: processing; ripeness of fruit; cooking; fat and protein and fibre content will all influence the rating.

One criticism of the glycaemic index is that some foods with a high GI may not necessarily contain a lot of carbohydrates, since the scale was formulated on a standard weight of carbohydrate (50g/2oz) and not based on an individual serving. For example, in the case of carrots, which contain only 7 per cent carbs, you would have to consume an unrealistic quantityto reach 50g/2oz carbohydrate content.

Consequently, the glycaemic load (GL) was created to take into account the amount of carbohydrate present in a single serving, and it is seen as a more balanced indicator of sugar content. You can, therefore, control your glycaemic response by eating low GI foods as well as by restricting your intake of carbs.

GI levels of added sugars:

Glucose	100
Regular sugar (sucrose)	65
Molasses	60
Honey	58
Maple syrup	54
Fructose	13–19
Agave syrup	11–19
Xylitol	7–13

READ THE LABEL

Food labels can be a minefield, especially when it comes to working out how much sugar a food contains. There are usually two figures for carbohydrates: 'Total carbohydrates xxg ...Of which sugars xxg". Look for the latter figure. Some manufacturers unhelpfully omit this information, often if the food is high in sugar! If so, take a look at the ingredients lists to see if sugars have been added.

The figure given on the nutritional panel is usually the amount of total sugars in the food. It may include natural sugars from fruit as well as added refined sugars. So a food containing lots of fruit could well be a healthier choice than one that contains lots of added sugars, even if the product contains a similar amount of total sugars. Check the ingredients list to see whether a food contains lots of added sugar or whether its sweetness comes from a natural source such as fruit.

Added sugar must be included in the ingredients list, which always starts with the largest ingredient first. Now sugar comes under many guises: anything ending in 'ose' can usually be assumed to be a sugar, including dextrose, sucrose, maltose, fructose, glucose, lactose and xylose, but there are others, such as corn syrup, corn sweetener, corn syrup solids, high fructose corn syrup, fruit concentrates and fruit syrup, invert sugars, honey, maltodextrin, maple syrup, molasses, dextrin, cane juice, malt syrup, raw sugar, rice syrup, sorghum, sorghum syrup, treacle, turbinado syrup and hydrolized starch.

SUGAR LEVELS – HIGH OR LOW?

According to UK government guidelines, a food that is high in sugar contains more than 15g/½oz sugars per 100g/3½oz, while a food low in sugar contains 5g/⅛oz or less per 100g/3½oz. If the amount of sugar per 100g/3½oz is in between these figures, that is a medium sugar level.

FOODS WITH ADDED SUGAR

Sugar can appear in the most unlikely of places – just think sauces, baked beans, cheese crackers, bread and ready meals. Furthermore, foods high in sugar are also likely to be high in fat, while contributing an excess of what is referred to as 'empty' calories. Here are some foods – some obvious, others less so – to look out for:

Baked Goods

Cakes
Biscuits (sweet and savoury)/cookies and crackers
Breads, brioche, crumpets, English muffins
Waffles and pancakes
Pastries, Danish pastries, apple turnovers, croissants, pies, fruit tarts
Cheesecakes
Cereal bars and flapjacks/bar cookies
Cake and batter mixes
Breakfast cereals
Flavoured rice cakes and oatcakes
Breadsticks

Canned Foods

Vegetables in sauce
Baked beans
Fish/meat in sauce
Spaghetti in tomato sauce
Pie fillings
Soups
Cooking sauces
Fruit in syrup
Sponge puddings, custard and rice pudding

Condiments

Oriental, Far Eastern and Middle Eastern sauces and pastes, soy sauce, barbecue sauce, tomato ketchup, pickles, salad dressings, mustard, mayonnaise, tomato paste, sandwich spreads, pesto

Gravy granules, stock cubes and liquid stock

Jams, marmalade, honey, molasses, maple syrup, fruit spreads, fruit compotes

Peanut butter

Dairy

Natural/flavoured yogurts, yogurt drinks, pro- and prebiotic drinks
Mousses, fools, crème caramel, tarts, ice cream
Flavoured cheese spreads, cheese snacks

Snack Foods and Beverages

Crisps/potato chips, pretzels
Cheese biscuits and crackers
Flavoured nuts
Dried fruit
Chocolates and sweets/candy
Chocolate drinks, malted drinks, fizzy drinks, fruit squashes,
   cordials, fruit juices and smoothies

Meat, Fish and Seafood

Pâtés, cured meats, sausages, sausage rolls
Ready meals
Burgers
Pies, pizza and flans
Breaded fish and meat
Processed potato products

ABOUT THE RECIPES

Many people follow a low-sugar diet because of health reasons, whether due to diabetes, hyperglycaemia, hypoglycaemia, insulin resistance or weight problems. The collection of recipes in this book takes this into account by following the principles of a nutritionally balanced diet. Basing your diet on these foods will help to keep blood-sugar levels steady, avoiding peaks and troughs, as well as providing you with the nutrients necessary for good health.

These easy-to-follow recipes are divided into six chapters: Basic Low-sugar Recipes, Breakfasts & Brunches, Light Meals & Snacks, Dinners, Desserts and Cakes, Bakes & Breads. Savoury foods can be surprisingly high in added sugar, particularly canned foods and sauces, and you'll find specially adapted recipes for healthier, low-sugar alternatives of these as well as the sweet treats we love.

Much use is made of fruit, cooked or otherwise. When baking, fruit will help to keep a cake moist as well as add natural sweetness, and spices such as nutmeg and cinnamon add aroma and flavour. Where necessary, but not to excess, fructose, xylitol and agave syrup are used. These natural sugar alternatives do not raise blood-sugar levels in the same way as regular sugar does.

Each recipe comes with an explanation of its health benefits, enabling you to create nutritionally balanced, low-sugar meals and to stick to the recommended figure of added sugar per day: **50g/1³/₄oz for women** and **70g/2¹/₂oz for men**. To help you calculate how much added sugar you eat on a daily basis, each recipe is accompanied by a nutritional analysis, which details calories and the carbohydrate count, including the amount of total sugar and the amount of added sugar, if applicable. Added sugars are those that are included in refined foods as well as in regular sugar, honey, syrups and molasses, etc.; they do not include sugars that are found naturally in fruit, for instance. This information will make it easier for you to cook sensibly with regard to sugar.

BASIC LOW-SUGAR RECIPES

Shop-bought sauces, relishes, jams and spreads can be notoriously high in sugar as well as containing a surprising number of additional ingredients such as fillers and additives. This collection of recipes provides sweet and savoury alternatives that are not only lower in sugar but are made with fresh ingredients.

All should be stored in the refrigerator in an airtight container.

Tomato Relish

Ditch the ketchup and opt instead for this refreshing, zingy relish that goes well with grilled/broiled meats, fish and poultry. It's also good spooned over brown rice or couscous. It is best served at room temperature.

SERVES 4   **PREPARATION** 10 minutes

4 vine-ripened tomatoes, quartered, deseeded and finely chopped

juice of 1 lime

1 red onion, finely chopped

1 mild green chilli, deseeded and finely chopped

1 small handful mint, finely chopped

salt and freshly ground black pepper

Put all the ingredients in a bowl and stir until well combined.

Mint Raita

Use this perfect cooling accompaniment to hot, spicy curries or tandoori meat and poultry in place of sugar-laden chutneys.

SERVES 4   **PREPARATION** 10 minutes

150ml/5fl oz/scant $^2/_3$ cup low-fat plain yogurt

10cm/4in piece cucumber, halved lengthways, deseeded and finely chopped

5 tbsp finely chopped mint

1 tsp fresh lemon juice

$^1/_2$ tsp cumin seeds

1 Put all the ingredients except for the cumin seeds in a bowl and stir until well combined.

2 Sprinkle the cumin seeds over the top before serving.

Tzatziki

This typical Greek appetizer is made with courgette instead of the usual cucumber. It can be served as a dip or as a cooling accompaniment to spicy dishes.

SERVES 4   **PREPARATION** 10 minutes

1 courgette/zucchini, trimmed and grated

1 small garlic clove, minced

150ml/5fl oz/scant ²/₃ cup 0% fat Greek yogurt

juice of ¹/₂ lemon

salt and freshly ground black pepper

Put all the ingredients in a bowl and stir until well combined.

Three-nut Butter

Sugar is an ingredient you least expect to find in peanut butter. By making your own nut butter, you can ensure it contains only the ingredients you want and no additives or added saturated fats. You can also use whatever combination of nuts you like. This butter can be stored in an airtight container in the refrigerator for up to 2 weeks.

MAKES 200g/7oz

PREPARATION 10 minutes   **COOKING** 5 minutes

50g/1³⁄₄oz/scant ¹⁄₂ cup almonds, shelled

50g/1³⁄₄oz/scant ¹⁄₂ cup unsalted cashew nuts

50g/1³⁄₄oz/scant ¹⁄₂ cup unsalted peanuts, shelled

90ml/3fl oz/generous ¹⁄₃ cup sunflower oil

salt, to taste

1   Toast the nuts in a dry frying pan for 4–5 minutes, turning once. If necessary, rub the nuts in a clean tea towel to remove the papery brown covering.

2   Transfer the nuts to a food processor or blender and process until finely ground. Pour in the oil and blend to a coarse paste, adding a little warm water if the mixture if very thick. Season with salt.

Date & Vanilla Spread

A spoonful of this rich spread is delicious on a wholemeal muffin or toast. It can also be served with yogurt, porridge/oatmeal or as a filling in pancakes. Dried dates do have a relatively high sugar content, but, because they are high in fibre, the sugars are broken down more slowly. Additionally, dates are a good source of iron, B-group vitamins, magnesium and potassium. This spread can be stored in an airtight container in the refrigerator for up to 2 weeks.

MAKES 270g/9½oz

PREPARATION 10 minutes   **COOKING** 20 minutes

200g/7oz/scant 2 cups chopped dried dates

1 tsp vanilla extract (optional)

1   Place the dates and 300ml/10½fl oz/1¼ cups water in a heavy-based saucepan. Bring to the boil, then reduce the heat and simmer, covered, for 20 minutes until the fruit is tender and most of the water has been absorbed.

2   Transfer the dates, and any remaining water, with the vanilla extract, if using, to a food processor or blender and blend until smooth. Set aside to cool before using.

Apricot & Prune Spread

Many jams have a surprisingly low fruit content and are high in added sugar. This healthier alternative contains considerably more fruit and less sugar, and is an excellent source of vitamins and minerals, especially iron. It's delicious spread on warm muffins or crumpets with low-fat cream cheese or fromage frais. This fruity spread can be stored in an airtight container in the refrigerator for up to 2 weeks

MAKES 350g/12oz

PREPARATION 10 minutes   **COOKING** 45 minutes

115g/4oz/^{1}/$_2$ cup unsulphured ready-to-eat dried apricots, roughly chopped

115g/4oz/^{1}/$_2$ cup ready-to-eat dried prunes, roughly chopped

1 Put the apricots and prunes in a non-metallic saucepan. Cover with 425ml/15fl oz/scant 1^3/$_4$ cups water and bring to the boil. Reduce the heat, cover, and simmer for 45 minutes until the fruit is very soft, swollen and almost caramelized.

2 Transfer the cooked fruit to a blender or food processor and blend with 75ml/2^1/$_2$fl oz/^{1}/$_3$ cup water to make a thick purée. Set aside to cool before using.

Strawberry Jam

Intensely fruity and fresh, this high-fruit, low-sugar jam is delicious spread on wholemeal toast, scones/biscuits or muffins. A spoonful can also be stirred into natural yogurt or used as a cake filling. This jam can be stored in an airtight container in the refrigerator for up to 1 week.

MAKES 300g/10½oz/2 cups

PREPARATION 5 minutes   **COOKING** 20 minutes

300g/10¹/₂oz/2 cups strawberries, hulled and halved

1 tbsp xylitol

1 tbsp fresh lemon juice

1   Wash the strawberries under cold running water and leave to drain. Put them in a saucepan with the xylitol and lemon juice and cook over a medium-low heat, stirring occasionally, for 5 minutes.

2   Remove the pan from the heat and mash the fruit with the back of a fork, then return to the heat and cook, half-covered, for 10–15 minutes until reduced and thickened – it should have a chunky syrupy texture. Set aside to cool before using.

BREAKFASTS & BRUNCHES

It may be a cliché, but breakfast is certainly the most important meal of the day, replenishing vital nutrients and energy depleted overnight. Recent research suggests that children who eat a decent breakfast perform better at school, and no doubt the same can be said of adults at work.

However, what you eat is equally as important as when. Eating, for example, a high-sugar cereal for breakfast leads to a temporary surge in blood glucose levels, which will be promptly followed by a mid-morning slump and subsequent hunger pangs and lull in energy levels. The following recipes enable you to ditch sugary refined cereals in favour of more sustaining and nutritious Cinnamon Porridge/Oatmeal with Pears, Blueberry & Almond Bircher Muesli or On-the-day Muesli, which is a healthy combination of nuts, fruits, seeds and oats and can literally be thrown together depending on what you have to hand.

There is also research to show that people who avoid breakfast pick on unhealthy snacks late morning, so if eating first thing is not really you then why not try the healthier Fruit & Nut Breakfast Bars or a pot of Plum & Oat Crunch?

For a more substantial savoury option, turn to the recipes for Baked Eggs & Spinach, Sardines & Tomato on Toast, or Cottage Cheese Pancakes to keep you going through to lunchtime.

Date & Vanilla Breakfast Yogurt

This thick and creamy fruit yogurt is a nourishing and energy-boosting blend of protein and slow-release carbohydrates, making it an excellent start to the day. Scatter over the chopped pistachio nuts just before serving for a delicious crunchy topping.

SERVES 4   **PREPARATION** 5 minutes   **COOKING** 17 minutes

40g/1¹/₂oz/¼ cup dried ready-to-eat stoned dates, roughly chopped

¹/₂ tsp vanilla extract

300ml/10¹/₂fl oz/1¼ cups thick natural low-fat bio yogurt

3 tbsp unsalted pistachio nuts, roughly chopped

1 Put the dates and 300ml/10 ¹/₂fl oz/1¼ cups water in a medium saucepan and bring to the boil, then reduce the heat and simmer, covered, for 15 minutes until the dates are very soft.

2 Mash the cooked dates with the back of a spoon or fork until puréed, then leave to cool slightly.

3 Stir the vanilla extract into the yogurt and divide the mixture into four tumblers or bowls. Add 1 heaped tablespoon of the date purée to each serving and stir in for a swirled effect. Scatter with the pistachio nuts before serving.

Storage

Can be stored in an airtight container in the refrigerator for up to 1 day. The date purée will keep for up to 5 days in the refrigerator.

Health Benefits

Dates make a nutritious natural sweetener, and their high-fibre content means that the sugars are released steadily into the body. However, it is best to eat dried fruit in moderation when following a low-sugar diet.

Food Facts per Portion

Calories 123kcal • Total Carbs 9.2g • total sugar 9.1g • added sugar 0g

Variations

Try swapping the dates for dried ready-to-eat apricots (the dark-coloured unsulphured variety have a wonderful rich toffee flavour).

In place of the pistachios, try roughly chopped walnuts, Brazils or brazils. Toasted sunflower or pumpkin seeds would also work.

Fruity French Toast

Ⓥ Ⓞ ⓐ Ⓘ ⓔ ⓢ ⓜ

This deliciously quick brunch would also make a great dessert. For a change, try swapping the berries for other types of fruit, such as nectarines, bananas or blueberries.

SERVES 4   **PREPARATION** 5 minutes   **COOKING** 5 minutes

2 large/extra-large eggs

4 tbsp skimmed milk

4 slices seeded wholemeal bread

20g/³⁄₄oz/4 tsp unsalted butter or polyunsaturated spread

sprinkling of cinnamon

4 tsp agave syrup

250g/9oz mixed berries of your choice, such as blueberries, strawberries, raspberries and blackberries (defrosted if frozen)

90ml/3fl oz/heaped ⅓ cup 0% fat Greek yogurt

1 Whisk the eggs and milk together in a shallow bowl. Dip both sides of each slice of bread in the egg mixture.

2 Melt the butter in a non-stick frying pan. Put the slices of egg-soaked bread in the pan and cook for 2 minutes on each side until golden.

3 Sprinkle the French toast with cinnamon and drizzle with agave syrup, then serve straightaway with the berries and yogurt on the side.

Health Benefits

Berries are little baubles of goodness and are a particularly rich source of antioxidants, including anthocyanins. These potent compounds are said to protect the body against the effect of ageing and improve circulation.

Food Facts per Portion

Calories 191kcal • Total Carbs 21.6g • total sugar 7.9g • added sugar 3.6g

Variation

Slices of banana, apple, pear or peach can be swapped for the mixed berries, if liked.

Vegetable Power Juice

If you like making fresh fruit juices, why not try a vegetable version for a change? This invigorating blend of colourful vegetables and fruit helps to support the immune system and provides a healthy dose of vitamins and minerals: the perfect start to the day.

SERVES 2   **PREPARATION** 5 minutes

2 sweet apples, quartered

1 small cucumber, halved lengthways

1 small fennel bulb, sliced into long wedges

¼ red cabbage, cored and sliced into long wedges

1 red bell pepper, quartered and deseeded

2.5cm/1in piece unpeeled fresh root ginger, halved lengthways

1 tbsp fresh lemon juice

1   Juice the apples, cucumber, fennel, cabbage, red bell pepper and ginger.

2   Add the lemon juice and stir the vegetable juice well until combined. Pour into glasses to serve.

Storage

Can be stored in an airtight container in the refrigerator for up to 12 hours. Stir before serving.

Health Benefits

Red cabbage and red bell pepper are a rich source of carotenoids. A diet rich in carotenoids, found in high amounts in yellow, orange and red fruit and vegetables, has been found to help those people with poor glucose tolerance.

Food Facts per Portion

Calories 51kcal • Total Carbs 11.3g • total sugar 11g • added sugar 0g

Variation

Juices are incredibly versatile and it is well worth experimenting with your own favourite combinations of fruit and vegetables as well as what is in season. Instead of the fennel and red cabbage you could try adding 2 carrots and 3 cooked beetroot and the juice of ½ lemon.

Banana & Peanut Butter Smoothie

Bananas and peanut butter may seem an unusual combination, but this smoothie provides plenty of energy for the morning ahead.

SERVES 2   **PREPARATION** 5 minutes

1 small ripe banana, thickly sliced

125ml/4fl oz/¹/₂ cup natural low-fat bio yogurt

350ml/12fl oz/scant 1¹/₂ cups semi-skimmed milk

1 heaped tbsp smooth, sugar-free peanut butter

¹/₂ tsp cinnamon

1   Place the banana, yogurt, milk, peanut butter and cinnamon in a blender.

2   Blend until smooth and frothy, then serve.

Storage

Can be stored in an airtight container in the refrigerator for up to 12 hours.

Health Benefits

Peanut butter contains valuable soluble fibre, which helps to slow down the absorption of sugars found in the bananas.

Food Facts per Portion

Calories 199kcal • Total Carbs 21.2g • total sugar 20.6g • added sugar 0g

Golden Grapefruit

Ⓥ Ⓖ

A refreshing, vitamin C boost to start the day. Pair the grapefruit with a poached egg on wholemeal toast for a nutritious and complete breakfast.

SERVES 2   **PREPARATION** 3 minutes   **COOKING** 4 minutes

1 red grapefruit, halved crossways

2 tsp pomegranate juice

1 Preheat the grill to medium and line the grill pan with foil. Cut into each grapefruit half with a small, sharp knife to loosen each segment.

2 Spoon the pomegranate juice over each grapefruit half. Cook for 3–4 minutes under the preheated grill until the grapefruit begins to caramelize on top, then serve immediately.

Health Benefits

Grapefruit, especially the pink and red ones, are rich in immune system-boosting antioxidants and also help to reduce harmful LDL cholesterol levels in the body. Eat regularly to reap the benefits of this super-fruit.

Food Facts per Portion

Calories 26kcal • Total Carbs 5.9g• total sugar 5.9g • added sugar 1.7g

Blueberry & Almond Bircher Muesli

Oats, apples and almonds provide fibre and slow-release energy to keep you going through the morning. This muesli is largely made the night before serving, which means you can save precious time in the morning.

SERVES 4   **PREPARATION** 10 minutes, plus soaking

200g/7oz/2 cups rolled oats

200ml/7fl oz/generous ¾ cup fresh apple juice (not from concentrate)

150ml/5fl oz/scant ⅔ cup semi-skimmed milk

170ml/5½fl oz/⅔ cup thick natural low-fat bio yogurt

2 sweet apples (unpeeled), cored and grated

1 large handful blueberries

1 heaped tbsp toasted flaked almonds

1 Put the oats in a mixing bowl and pour the apple juice over. Cover with cling film and leave in the refrigerator overnight.

2 Just before serving, stir in the milk, yogurt and grated apple. Spoon into four bowls and top with the blueberries and almonds before serving.

Storage

The oat and apple juice mixture can be stored in an airtight container in the refrigerator for up to 1 day.

Health Benefits

Blueberries are high in beneficial antioxidants and they provide significant amounts of vitamins C and E, which support the immune system. Especially good for the eyes, blueberries help to protect against macular degeneration. The soluble fibre found in oats helps to balance blood-sugar levels, whilst the almonds, yogurt and milk provide valuable amounts of bone-strengthening calcium.

Food Facts per Portion

Calories 362kcal • Total Carbs 47.2g • total sugar 16.2g • added sugar 0g

On-the-day Muesli

Ⓥ ❷ ❸ ❹ ❺

The beauty of making your own muesli is that you can add your favourite fruit, nuts and seeds, or whatever you have to hand. If strawberries are out of season, try pomegranate seeds or chopped pear or apple.

SERVES 1   **PREPARATION** 10 minutes

3 tbsp whole oats

1 unsulphured, ready-to-eat dried apricot, chopped

1 tbsp sunflower seeds

1 tbsp pumpkin seeds

1 tsp hemp seeds

2 Brazil nuts, chopped

2 walnuts, broken into pieces

4 heaped tbsp natural low-fat bio yogurt

75ml/2^{1}/$_{2}$fl oz/^{1}/$_{3}$ cup oat milk

2 strawberries, hulled and halved or quartered, or other fruit

1 Put the oats, apricots, seeds and nuts in a serving bowl. Add the yogurt and milk and mix until combined.

2 Top with the strawberries and serve.

Storage

The muesli mixture can be stored in an airtight container for up to 1 week.

Health Benefits

Pumpkin seeds and walnuts are two of the few non-fish sources of omega-3 fats, which benefit the eyes, brain and skin. Sunflower seeds are also brimming with selenium and vitamin E.

Food Facts per Portion

Calories 583kcal • Total Carbs 48.2g• total sugar 14.7g • added sugar 0g

Cinnamon Porridge/Oatmeal with Pears

Ⓥ Ⓐ Ⓒ Ⓓ Ⓔ Ⓕ

Full of valuable soluble fibre, vitamins and minerals, this dish is wonderfully comforting and sustaining, whilst the chopped pears add natural sweetness along with vitamin C and antioxidants.

SERVES 4   **PREPARATION** 5 minutes   **COOKING** 12–17 minutes

200g/7oz/scant 2 cups whole oats

600ml/21fl oz/scant 2½ cups semi-skimmed milk

2 tsp cinnamon

1 ripe pear, cored and chopped

16 walnut halves, broken

1 heaped tbsp toasted sunflower seeds

2 tsp agave syrup

1   Put the oats in a saucepan with the milk, cinnamon and 800ml/28fl oz/3¼ cups water. Bring to the boil, then reduce the heat and simmer, half-covered, for 10–15 minutes until thickened, stirring frequently.

2   To serve, divide the porridge/oatmeal between four bowls, then spoon over the chopped pear. Scatter with the walnut halves and sunflower seeds. Drizzle with the agave syrup before serving.

Health Benefits

Oats are high in soluble fibre, which helps to regulate levels of cholesterol and blood glucose in the body. Surprisingly, cinnamon also plays a role in balancing blood-sugar levels, behaving in a similar way to the hormone insulin.

Food Facts per Portion

Calories 396kcal • Total Carbs 45g • total sugar 12.8g • added sugar 1.8g

Variation

Bananas and apples would also make a delicious fruity topping for porridge/oatmeal, in place of the pears.

Plum & Oat Crunch

V ⊳ ⊘ ⊜ ⊕

This quick version of the crunchy breakfast cereal granola is mixed with low-fat Greek yogurt and juicy plums to make a nutritious breakfast. Alternatively, it could be served as a quick and simple dessert.

SERVES 4   **PREPARATION** 15 minutes   **COOKING** 7 minutes

115g/4oz/1 cup whole oats

90ml/3fl oz/heaped ⅓ cup sunflower seeds

90ml/3fl oz/heaped ⅓ cup pumpkin seeds

2 tbsp agave syrup

8 ripe plums, halved, stoned and chopped

300ml/10½fl oz/1¼ cups 2% fat Greek yogurt

1 Put the oats in a frying pan and dry-fry over a medium-low heat, turning them occasionally, for 5 minutes. Add the sunflower and pumpkin seeds and dry-fry for another 2 minutes, stirring regularly, until light golden.

2 Take the pan off the heat and add the agave syrup. Stir until the oats and seeds are coated in the syrup. Leave to cool.

3 Divide half the oat mixture between four glasses, then divide half the plums over the top, then half the yogurt. Add another layer of each.

Storage
The oat and seed mixture can be stored in an airtight container for up to 5 days.

Health Benefits
Early research shows that certain substances found in plums may be able to decrease blood-glucose levels in the body.

Food Facts per Portion
Calories 461kcal • Total Carbs 39g • total sugar 11.1g • added sugar 5.5g

Banana Griddle Cakes

Banana helps to add a touch of sweetness to these griddle cakes, replacing the need for refined sugar. Serve sprinkled with fresh berries for added sweetness.

SERVES 4   **PREPARATION** 25 minutes   **COOKING** 10–14 minutes

140g/5oz/1¼ cups self-raising wholemeal flour

1 tsp baking soda

200ml/7 fl oz/generous ¾ cup semi-skimmed milk

1 egg, lightly beaten

2 heaped tbsp natural low-fat bio yogurt

1 large, ripe banana, mashed

sunflower oil, for frying

To serve:

6 heaped tbsp low-fat fromage frais

mixed berries

1   Sift the flour (adding any bran left in the sifter) and baking soda into a mixing bowl and make a well in the centre.

2   Whisk the milk with the egg, then gradually pour it into flour, whisking constantly to avoid any lumps. Stir in the yogurt and set aside for 15 minutes, then stir in the mashed banana.

3 Heat a flat griddle or large non-stick frying pan, then dip a
scrunched-up piece of kitchen roll into the oil and carefully
wipe a little over the pan. Spoon 3 tablespoons of the batter
per cake into the pan, cooking 3 cakes at a time, and cook for
about 1–1½ minutes on each side until golden. Remove and
keep warm, then re-oil the pan before cooking the remaining
3 batches of cakes to make a total of 12.

4 Serve the warm griddle cakes with a spoonful of fromage
frais and some berries.

Storage

The griddle cakes can be stored in an airtight container in the
refrigerator for up to 1 day, then reheated.

Health Benefits

The fibre found in wholemeal flour and bananas helps to slow
the digestion and absorption of carbohydrates, including sugars, in
the body, which means that blood-glucose levels remain stable
after eating.

Food Facts per Portion

Calories 227kcal • Total Carbs 33.2g • total sugar 12.9g • added sugar 0g

Fruit & Nut Breakfast Bars

Packed with protein-rich nuts and seeds as well as energy-giving, iron-boosting dried fruit, one of these simple-to-prepare breakfast bars would also make an excellent snack. Serve with a bowl of natural yogurt.

MAKES 12 bars

PREPARATION 15 minutes, plus chilling   **COOKING** 3–5 minutes

25g/1oz/¼ cup hazelnuts, roughly chopped

25g/1oz/¼ cup cashew nuts, roughly chopped

50g/1¾oz/½ cup whole oats

2 tbsp sunflower seeds

2 tbsp pumpkin seeds

100g/3½oz/¾ cup raisins

150g/5½oz/scant ¾ cup unsulphured ready-to-eat dried apricots, cut into small pieces

4 tbsp fresh orange juice

1 Put the hazelnuts, cashew nuts and oats in a dry frying pan and toast over a medium heat for 3–5 minutes, turning them occasionally with a wooden spatula until they begin to turn golden and the oats become crisp. Remove from the heat and leave to cool.

2 Put the nuts, oats and seeds in a food processor or blender and process until they are very finely chopped. Tip the nut mixture into a bowl.

3 Put the raisins, apricots and orange juice into the food processor or blender and purée until the mixture becomes a smooth, thick purée. Scrape the fruit purée into the mixing bowl and stir into the nut mixture.

4 Line an 18 x 25cm/7 x 10in baking tin with parchment paper. Tip the mixture into the tin and, using a palette knife, smooth into an even layer, about 1cm/½in thick. Chill for 1 hour before cutting into 12 bars.

Storage
Can be stored in an airtight container for up to 5 days.

Health Benefits
Dried fruit is high in natural sugars but, unlike refined sugars, it also provides valuable fibre and nutrients, particularly the mineral iron. The oats, nuts and seeds will all help to slow down the absorption of natural sugars from the dried fruit.

Food Facts per Portion
Calories 115kcal • Total carbs 14.8g • total sugar 10.9g • added sugar 0g

Cheese & Tomato Soufflés

Ⓥ Ⓞ 🍞

If you find the idea of making a soufflé a little off-putting, this version really couldn't be easier, and a hollowed-out tomato makes the perfect container. Serve with seeded bread or toast.

SERVES 4   **PREPARATION** 20 minutes   **COOKING** 20–25 minutes

4 large beefsteak tomatoes, top 5mm/¼in sliced off

90ml/3fl oz/generous ⅓ cup semi-skimmed milk

2 large garlic cloves, minced

4 eggs, separated

100g/3½oz/¾ cup grated strong half-fat Cheddar cheese

1 tsp olive oil

salt and freshly ground black pepper

snipped chives, to sprinkle (optional)

1   Preheat the oven to 190°C/375°F/Gas Mark 5. Scoop out the seeds of the tomatoes to make an empty shell. Sprinkle the inside of the tomatoes with salt and place upside-down on a plate. Set aside for 10 minutes, then rinse and pat dry with kitchen towels.

2   Meanwhile, gently heat the milk until just warm, then stir in the garlic and egg yolks and three-quarters of the Cheddar. Heat gently, stirring, until the cheese has melted and the mixture thickened. Remove from the heat and season.

3 Whisk the egg whites in a grease-free bowl until they form stiff peaks. Using a metal spoon, stir a spoonful of the whites into the egg yolk mixture to slacken it, then fold in the remaining egg whites until they are well combined.

4 Grease an ovenproof dish with the olive oil and place the tomatoes upright in the dish. Spoon the soufflé mixture into the tomatoes and sprinkle with the remaining cheese. Bake in the preheated oven for 15–20 minutes until the soufflés have risen and are light golden on top. Remove from the oven and sprinkle with chives, if using, then serve.

Health Benefits

Eggs provide good-quality protein, which is essential for growth and development, such as the production of hormones, enzymes and antibodies. Tomatoes are rich in lycopene (which gives the fruit its red colour), which can protect against cancer.

Food Facts per Portion

Calories 172kcal • Total Carbs 3.1g • total sugar 3g • added sugar 0g

Kedgeree

This nutritionally balanced breakfast provides a useful combination of complex carbohydrates, protein, vitamins and minerals.

SERVES 4   **PREPARATION** 15 minutes   **COOKING** 30–35 minutes

200g/7oz/1 cup brown basmati rice

2 bay leaves

2 tsp low-salt bouillon powder

500g/1lb 2oz undyed smoked haddock fillets

2 tbsp sunflower oil

1 large onion, chopped

2 tsp black mustard seeds

150g/5$^{1}/_{2}$oz/1$^{1}/_{2}$ cups spinach leaves, tough stalks removed

4$^{1}/_{2}$ tsp garam masala

4 green cardamom pods, split

2 tsp ground turmeric

25g/1oz/4$^{1}/_{2}$ tsp unsalted butter or polyunsaturated spread

4 hard-boiled eggs

freshly ground black pepper

1 Put the rice in a saucepan and pour in sufficient water to cover it by 1cm/$^{1}/_{2}$in. Add the bay leaves and bring to the boil. Stir in the bouillon powder, then reduce the heat to its lowest setting.

2 Cover the pan with a lid and simmer over the lowest heat for 25–30 minutes until the water has been absorbed and the rice is tender. Remove the pan from the heat and leave to stand, covered, for 5 minutes.

3 Meanwhile, put the fish in a large sauté pan and cover with water. Bring to the boil, then reduce the heat and simmer for 3–5 minutes until cooked. Using a fish slice, take the fish out of the water (reserving 90ml/3fl oz/generous ⅓ cup), remove the skin and any bones and flake the fish into large chunks.

4 Heat the oil in the cleaned pan and fry the onion for 8 minutes until softened, then stir in the mustards seeds for 1 minute. Add the spinach and remaining spices and cook for 2 minutes, adding the reserved cooking water. Stir in the rice, haddock and butter and turn gently until heated through. Season to taste. Halve the eggs and arrange them on top before serving.

Storage
The rice can be stored in an airtight container in the refrigerator for up to 2 days, then reheated thoroughly with the onion mixture.

Health Benefits
Brown rice provides higher levels of fibre and nutrients, such as vitamins B, manganese, magnesium and iron, than white rice.

Food Facts per Portion
Calories 468kcal • Total Carbs 40.1g • total sugar 2g • added sugar 0g

Home-made Baked Beans

Tinned baked beans often contain excessive amounts of sugar and salt, so by making your own you can control which ingredients you use and keep sugar levels to a minimum.

SERVES 4   **PREPARATION** 5 minutes   **COOKING** 25 minutes

2 tbsp olive oil

1 onion, grated

1 large garlic clove, minced

400g/14oz tinned haricot beans in water, drained and rinsed

300ml/10¹/₂fl oz/1¹/₄ cups passata (sieved tomatoes)

1 tsp English mustard powder

1 tbsp vegetarian Worcestershire sauce

1 tbsp blackstrap molasses

1 tbsp tomato paste

salt and freshly ground black pepper

1   Heat the oil in a saucepan and fry the onion for 8 minutes, stirring occasionally. Add the garlic and cook for another minute or until the onion has softened.

2   Pour in the beans and passata, then add the English mustard powder, Worcestershire sauce, molasses, tomato paste and 4 tablespoons water and stir until combined.

3 Bring to the boil, then reduce the heat and simmer, half-covered, for 10 minutes until the sauce has reduced and thickened. Season to taste, then serve hot.

Storage

Can be stored in an airtight container in the refrigerator for up to 3 days, then reheated.

Health Benefits

Haricot beans are a great source of heart-friendly B vitamins and folate. These help to reduce homocysteine levels, high amounts of which increase the risk of heart disease. The rich, dark blackstrap molasses is a good source of iron, calcium, magnesium, potassium and zinc.

Food Facts per Portion

Calories 150kcal • Total Carbs 17.9g • total sugar 6.6g • added sugar 2.1g

Baked Eggs & Spinach

Ⓥ Ⓞ ⊜

These individual eggs Florentine can partly be prepared in advance to save time in the morning: follow steps 1–2, then cover the ramekins and chill overnight. Serve with wholemeal toast.

SERVES 4   **PREPARATION** 10 minutes   **COOKING** 5 minutes

500g/1lb 2oz/5½ cups young leaf spinach, tough stalks removed, rinsed well

3 tbsp half-fat créme fraîche

a little grated nutmeg

4 eggs

55g/2oz/½ cup grated strong half-fat Cheddar cheese

salt and freshly ground black pepper

1   Steam the spinach for 2 minutes until wilted. Leave to drain, then squeeze out any excess water using your hands.

2   Finely chop the spinach, then mix with the crème fraîche and a little grated nutmeg. Season and spoon the spinach mixture into four large ramekins.

3   Preheat the grill to medium. Break an egg into each ramekin and sprinkle with cheese. Place the ramekins in the grill pan and cook under the preheated grill for 2–3 minutes until the eggs are just set, then serve straightaway.

Storage

The pre-cooked egg mixture can be stored in an airtight container in the refrigerator for up to 1 day, then cooked.

Health Benefits

Dark leafy vegetables, such as spinach, are an important source of cancer-fighting antioxidants. Spinach also contains fibre, which can help to reduce harmful levels of LDL cholesterol, so reducing the risk of heart disease and strokes. Its vitamin C content helps the absorption of the iron that is also present.

Food Facts per Portion

Calories 163kcal • Total Carbs 2.3g • total sugar 2.2g • added sugar 0g

Cottage Cheese Pancakes

These pancakes are given a protein boost thanks to the addition of cottage cheese. They come served with a fresh tomato and basil salad, but if you prefer something warmer, the homemade baked beans (see page 50) go particularly well with them. Serve one or two pancakes per person, depending on appetite.

SERVES 2–4   **PREPARATION** 20 minutes   **COOKING** 12 minutes

30g/1oz/¼ cup plain/all-purpose wholemeal flour

15g/½oz/1 tbsp unsalted butter, softened, or polyunsaturated spread

70g/2½oz/heaped ¼ cup cottage cheese

2 eggs

2 tbsp semi-skimmed milk

sunflower oil, for frying

40g/1½oz/scant ½ cup strong half-fat Cheddar cheese, grated

½ tsp fresh lemon juice

4 vine-ripened tomatoes, sliced

1 small handful basil leaves

salt and freshly ground black pepper

1   Sift the flour (adding any bran left in the sieve) into a blender, add the butter, cottage cheese, eggs and milk and whizz to make a batter. Season and leave to rest for 15 minutes.

2   Dip a scrunched-up piece of kitchen paper into the oil and
    wipe a little over a heavy-based frying pan, then heat the pan.
    Pour a quarter of the batter into the pan and swirl the pan
    until the batter coats the base.

3   Cook the pancake for about 2 minutes, then sprinkle a quarter
    of the Cheddar over one side. Fold the pancake in half and cook
    for another minute. Remove from the pan and keep warm while
    you cook the 3 remaining pancakes, re-oiling in between.

4   Squeeze the lemon juice over the tomatoes, season and top
    with the basil leaves. Serve the pancakes straightaway with
    the tomato salad.

Health Benefits

Cheese provides valuable calcium, which maintains healthy bones
and teeth. The mineral is also required for nerve and muscle
function. However, dairy produce can be high in saturated fat, so
using low-fat versions such as cottage cheese is a good idea.

Food Facts per Portion

Calories 159kcal • Total Carbs 6.6g • total sugar 2.4g • added sugar 0g

Sardines & Tomato on Toast

Economical and nutritious, tinned fish makes a useful store-cupboard standby. This dish can be rustled up in minutes.

SERVES 1   **PREPARATION** 5 minutes   **COOKING** 5 minutes

1 slice seeded wholemeal bread

2 tinned sardines in olive oil, spine removed

1 vine-ripened tomato, quartered, deseeded and chopped

pinch of crushed dried chillies

4 basil leaves, torn

1   Preheat the grill to medium-high. Toast the bread on one side.

2   Drain the sardines and mash lightly with a fork, then combine with the chopped tomato.

3   Spoon the sardine mixture on top of the non-toasted side of the bread and sprinkle over the crushed chillies. Grill for 3 minutes under the preheated grill, scatter with the basil and serve.

Health Benefits

Our heart, eyes, brain and metabolism all benefit from the omega-3 fats found in oily fish such as sardines.

Food Facts per Portion

Calories 187kcal • Total Carbs 13.6g • total sugar 2.8g • added sugar 0g

LIGHT MEALS & SNACKS

Low-sugar diets are not just about reducing the amount of sugar you eat but also about cutting your intake of refined carbohydrates such as crisps, pizza, white bread, white rice, white pasta, breaded meats and other processed foods. These foods often form the basis of snacks and light meals, yet unfortunately have a similar negative affect on blood-sugar levels as those foods that are high in sugar, causing peaks and troughs in energy levels. What's more, many processed savoury snacks are often high in fat and salt, and, somewhat surprisingly, may contain added sugar, too.

A couple of nutritious snacks a day will help to sustain energy, aid concentration and prevent mood swings. Choose from the quick and easy Soy Nuts & Seeds, Indian-spiced Roasted Pulses or Pitta Pizzas, made with a wholemeal base.

The light meals, too, are all simple to make – just right when you don't have a lot of time on your hands – and make the most of wholegrains, pulses and vegetables, such as the vibrant Warm Greek Salad of Beans, Basil & Feta, spicy Huevos Rancheros and warming Vegetable & Chicken Ramen.

Soy Nuts & Seeds

Whilst nuts tend to be relatively high in fat, it is generally the healthy unsaturated type. They are also a good source of protein, selenium, iron and fibre. A small handful – about 30g/1oz – is a good snack serving size. Use tamari instead of soy sauce if you want a wheat- and gluten-free nibble. Note that some makes of soy sauce contain added sugar, so it's a good idea to check the label before buying to avoid, if possible.

SERVES 6   **PREPARATION** 5 minutes   **COOKING** 8–10 minutes

185g/6½oz/ heaped 1 cup mixed unsalted nuts and seeds such as
    walnuts, Brazils, almonds, cashews, hazelnuts, sunflower seeds
    and pumpkin seeds

1 tbsp reduced-salt soy sauce (no added sugar)

1   Preheat the oven to 160°C/315°F/Gas 3. Place your chosen selection of nuts on a baking tray and roast in the preheated oven for about 6 minutes.

2   Add the seeds and turn until combined, then roast for another 2–4 minutes until they smell toasted and are light golden. Keep an eye on them because they can burn easily.

3   Remove the nuts and seeds from the oven and transfer them to a bowl. Leave to cool slightly, then drizzle the soy sauce over the top and turn the nuts and seeds with a spoon until they are coated all over. Serve.

Storage

Can be stored in an airtight container for up to 1 week.

Health Benefits

Pumpkin seeds are one of the few foods that provide useful amounts of both healthy omega-3 and omega-6 fats. They are also a good source of iron – essential for new blood cells – and zinc, which benefits the health of the skin, hair and nails.

Food Facts per Portion

Calories 188kcal • Total Carbs 3.4g • total sugar 1g • added sugar 0g

Variation

For spicy nuts and seeds, replace the soy sauce with a spice mix of your choice – Cajun spices are particularly good. After the nuts and seeds have been toasted, transfer them to a bowl and sprinkle over 1 tsp Cajun spice blend. Using a spoon, turn the nuts and seeds until coated.

Indian-spiced Pulses

Chickpeas/garbanzo beans, when roasted, make tasty, crunchy little snacks, and are lower in fat than nuts or crisps. Carotina oil gives a wonderful golden colour to the pulses, but you could use olive oil instead.

SERVES 4   PREPARATION 10 minutes   COOKING 1 hour

400g/14oz tinned chickpeas/garbanzo beans in water, drained and rinsed

1 tbsp carotina oil or olive oil

1/2 tsp low-sodium salt

1 1/2–2 tsp tandoori spice mix

1   Preheat the oven to 170°C/325°F/Gas 3. Line a plate with kitchen paper and pour the pulses on top. Pat dry with another sheet of kitchen paper.

2   Tip the pulses into a bowl and add the oil, salt and tandoori spice mix. Stir until the pulses are coated in the spicy oil mix.

3   Spread the pulses over a baking sheet in an even layer and roast in the preheated oven for 1 hour or until crisp, turning them occasionally. Remove from the oven and leave to cool before serving.

Storage

Can be stored in an airtight container for up to 3 days.

Health Benefits

Chickpeas/garbanzo beans, like other pulses, are high in soluble fibre, stabilize blood-sugar levels and help to lower cholesterol. Their potassium content helps to balance body fluids.

Carotina oil is a combination of red palm oil and canola oil and provides more vitamin E (as well as omega-3 and omega-6) than other types of oil.

Food Facts per Portion

Calories 113kcal • Total Carbs 11.2g • total sugar 0.3g • added sugar 0g

Pitta Pizzas

These pizzas couldn't be more simple or quick to make and always go down well with kids. Try adding your favourite toppings – see below for ideas – and serve with vegetable crudités or a mixed salad.

SERVES 4   **PREPARATION** 5 minutes   **COOKING** 8–10 minutes

5 tbsp passata (sieved tomatoes) or chopped tomatoes

1 small garlic clove, minced

2 tsp tomato paste

1 tsp dried oregano

4 wholemeal pitta breads

150g/5^1/$_2$oz reduced-fat mozzarella cheese, torn into pieces

16 pitted black olives, sliced

1–2 tsp olive oil

salt and freshly ground black pepper

1   Preheat the grill to medium-high and line the grill pan with foil. Mix together the passata, garlic, paste and oregano.

2   Spread the tomato sauce over the top of each pitta bread, then sprinkle with the mozzarella. Scatter the olives over the top.

3   Drizzle a little olive oil over each pizza and season to taste. Grill the pizzas under the preheated grill for 8–10 minutes until the mozzarella is bubbling and golden, then serve.

Health Benefits

Make sure olive oil plays a regular part in your diet, since it has been shown to improve the way glucose is absorbed by the cells and also helps to reduce blood pressure.

Food Facts per Portion

Calories 305kcal • Total Carbs 39g • total sugar 3.2g • added sugar 0g

Variations

Boost the vegetable content of the pizzas by topping them with slices of onion, mushroom or sweet bell peppers. You could also add pepperoni, salami or ham.

Tomato & Lentil Soup

Tinned tomato soup contains a surprising amount of added sugar, unlike this homemade version, which features the added health benefit of lentils. Serve the soup with slices of crusty wholemeal bread.

SERVES 4   **PREPARATION** 15 minutes   **COOKING** 40 minutes

1 tbsp olive oil

1 large onion, chopped

1 large carrot, peeled and finely chopped

2 celery sticks, finely chopped

500ml/17fl oz/2 cups passata (sieved tomatoes)

500ml/17fl oz/2 cups low-salt vegetable bouillon

55g/2oz/¼ cup split red lentils, rinsed

1 bay leaf

1 bouquet garni

salt and freshly ground black pepper

2 tbsp half-fat crème fraîche, to serve (optional)

1   Heat the oil in a large, heavy-based saucepan. Add the onion, cover the pan and sauté for 5 minutes until softened and transparent. Add the carrot and celery, cover, and cook for a further 3 minutes, stirring occasionally to prevent the vegetables sticking to the bottom of the pan.

2 Add the passata, bouillon, lentils, bay leaf and bouquet garni and bring to the boil, then reduce the heat and simmer, half-covered, for 30 minutes until the lentils and vegetables are tender and the soup has thickened.

3 Remove the bay leaf and bouquet garni. Using a stick blender, purée the soup until smooth. Season to taste and serve in four bowls topped with a spoonful of crème fraîche, if using.

Storage

Can be stored in an airtight container in the refrigerator for up to 3 days or the freezer for up to 3 months, then reheated.

Health Benefits

The lentil is much underused and underrated, but this humble pulse is bursting with nutrients, including B vitamins, which aid the release of energy from foods, and valuable fibre.

Food Facts per Portion

Calories 130kcal • Total Carbs 16.8g • total sugar 8.2g • added sugar 0g

Warm Greek Salad of Beans, Basil & Feta

Toss aside your memories of butter beans from school days, as this warm salad is in a different league. The cream-coloured butter bean is flavoured with garlic, herbs, tomatoes and lemon to make a salad that is full of Mediterranean flavours.

SERVES 4   **PREPARATION** 10 minutes   **COOKING** 5 minutes

2 tbsp extra-virgin olive oil

3 large garlic cloves, chopped

1 large red bell pepper, halved, deseeded and diced

800g/1lb 12oz tinned butter beans in water, drained and rinsed

2 tsp dried oregano

10 spring onions/scallions, sliced

12 cherry tomatoes, halved

juice of 1 lemon

185g/6½oz reduced-fat feta cheese, cubed

1 large handful basil leaves, torn

salt and freshly ground black pepper

1   Heat the oil in a frying pan and fry the garlic and pepper for 1 minute. Add the beans, oregano, spring onions/scallions and tomatoes and stir gently, then cook for another minute.

2   Stir in the lemon juice and heat through, then season to taste.
    Divide among four plates and top with the feta. Scatter the
    basil leaves over the top before serving.

Storage

Can be stored in an airtight container in the refrigerator for up to
2 days.

Health Benefits

Although much maligned, tinned pulses make a useful and
nutritious addition to the store cupboard. Butter beans provide both
types of fibre: soluble (good for the heart) and insoluble (good
for the bowel). Basil is said to be good for the digestion, easing
constipation.

Food Facts per Portion

Calories 292kcal • Total Carbs 20.8g • total sugar 3.7g • added sugar 0g

Red Quinoa Tabbouleh

Serve this herby salad at room temperature with the slices of freshly char-grilled halloumi placed on top. Halloumi tastes best when served warm straight after cooking.

SERVES 4   **PREPARATION** 20 minutes   **COOKING** 16 minutes

125g/4¹/₂oz/²/₃ cup red quinoa

6 vine-ripened tomatoes, deseeded and cut into bite-sized pieces

7 spring onions/scallions, sliced

1 small cucumber, halved, deseeded and diced

35g/1¹/₄oz mint, chopped

35g/1¹/₄oz flat leaf parsley, chopped

juice of 1 lemon

¹/₂ tsp crushed dried chillies (optional)

250g/9oz halloumi light, sliced

1 tbsp olive oil

salt and freshly ground black pepper

1   Put the quinoa in a saucepan and cover with boiling water. Bring to the boil, then reduce the heat and simmer, covered, for about 10 minutes or until tender. Drain the quinoa, put it in a serving bowl and leave to cool.

2   Add the tomatoes, spring onions/scallions, cucumber, mint and parsley. Squeeze in the lemon juice, add the crushed chillies, if using, and season well. Stir until combined.

3   Heat a griddle pan or frying pan. Brush the halloumi with the oil and cook for 4 minutes or until slightly golden. Divide the tabbouleh among four plates, top with the halloumi and serve.

Storage

The tabbouleh can be stored in an airtight container in the refrigerator for up to 2 days.

Health Benefits

Like golden quinoa, the red variety is a source of complete protein, providing about the same amount as milk and double that of rice. But that's not all – quinoa is also gluten free, low GI and low in fat, a good source of omega-6 and packed with minerals and B vitamins, so the grain makes a great contribution to a healthy diet.

Food Facts per Portion

Calories 155kcal • Total Carbs 21.7g • total sugar 6.9g • added sugar 0g

Avocado & Tomato Bruschetta

This is a simple and delicious combination, but make sure the tomatoes and avocado are nice and ripe for the best flavour. For a light lunch, serve with a crisp green salad.

SERVES 2   **PREPARATION** 7 minutes   **COOKING** 3 minutes

2 thickly cut slices of soda bread

1 small avocado, halved and pitted

1 vine-ripened tomato, sliced into rounds

$\frac{1}{2}$ tsp balsamic vinegar or fresh lemon juice

$\frac{1}{2}$ tsp extra-virgin olive oil

4 large basil leaves

freshly ground black pepper

1   Toast the soda bread on both sides.

2   Meanwhile, scoop the avocado flesh out of its skin with a spoon into a bowl, then mash with a fork. Spoon the avocado straight onto the toast – there's no need for any butter.

3   Top the avocado with the slices of tomato and drizzle with the balsamic vinegar and olive oil. Season with pepper to taste, scatter with the basil leaves and serve.

Health Benefits

Lycopene, the plant compound found in rich amounts in tomatoes, is more readily absorbed by the body when the tomato is cooked. Lycopene has been found to protect us from certain cancers and heart disease.

Food Facts per Portion

Calories 194kcal • Total Carbs 17.5g • total sugar 2.4g • added sugar 0g

Variation

Ricotta, humous or sliced mozzarella would all make delicious replacements for the avocado.

Spicy Tofu Cakes with Dipping Sauce

Tofu really benefits from being combined with more intense flavours, such as herbs and spices. These savoury patties make a light meal served with the dip and a cucumber and onion salad, or, for something a little more substantial, serve with a soba noodle salad.

SERVES 4

PREPARATION 20 minutes, plus chilling   **COOKING** 10–14 minutes

500g/1lb 2oz block firm tofu, drained

2 tbsp curry paste of your choice

2 large garlic cloves, minced

2.5cm/1in piece fresh root ginger, peeled and grated

1 red chilli, deseeded and finely chopped

4 tbsp chopped coriander/cilantro leaves

4 spring onions/scallions, finely chopped

3 tbsp plain/all-purpose flour, plus extra for dusting

2 tbsp sunflower oil

salt and freshly ground black pepper

Dipping sauce:

125ml/4fl oz/½ cup natural low-fat bio yogurt

2 tsp fresh lemon juice

2 tbsp chopped mint

1   Pat the tofu dry with kitchen paper, then coarsely grate into a bowl. Add the curry paste, garlic, ginger, chilli, coriander/cilantro and spring onions/scallions. Sift in the flour and a little salt and mix to make a coarse, sticky paste. Cover and refrigerate for 1 hour for the flavours to infuse and to allow the mixture to firm up slightly.

2   Meanwhile, make the dipping sauce by mixing together the yogurt, lemon juice and mint in a bowl, then season to taste.

3   Take large walnut-sized balls of the mixture and, using floured hands, flatten into rounds until you have 12 patties.

4   Heat the oil in a large frying pan and cook the tofu cakes in 2 batches for 4–6 minutes, turning once, until golden. Keep the first batch warm while you cook the second one. Drain on kitchen paper and serve warm with the dipping sauce.

Health Benefits

Tofu is a curd made from fermented soya milk and is often referred to as a super-food because of its numerous health benefits. Rich in minerals, particularly iron and calcium, it is also low in saturated fat and cholesterol-free. It has been found to help reduce blood pressure and blood cholesterol and the risk of certain cancers.

Food Facts per Portion

Calories 213kcal • Total Carbs 12.5g • total sugar 1.1g • added sugar 0g

Huevos Rancheros

Traditionally served for breakfast, this Tex-Mex dish makes a simple light meal when served with a large green salad.

SERVES 4   **PREPARATION** 15 minutes   **COOKING** 20–25 minutes

3 tbsp olive oil

1 large onion, chopped

1 green bell pepper, halved, deseeded and sliced

1 large garlic clove, chopped

2 tsp ground cumin

1/2 tsp chilli powder (optional)

2 tsp dried oregano

800g/1lb 12oz/3 1/3 cups tinned chopped tomatoes

200g/7oz tinned kidney beans in water, drained and rinsed

4 eggs

4 soft wholemeal tortillas

salt and freshly ground black pepper

1   Heat half of the olive oil in a frying pan. Add the onion and fry gently for 5 minutes, stirring regularly. Add the pepper and cook for 3 minutes, then stir in the garlic and fry for a further 1 minute.

2   Stir in the cumin, chilli powder, if using, oregano, tomatoes and kidney beans and bring to the boil, then simmer for 10–15 minutes until reduced and thickened. Season to taste.

3   Meanwhile, heat the remaining oil in a large frying pan. Break the eggs into the pan and fry until cooked. Warm the tortillas following the packet instructions and top each one with a quarter of the tomato and bean sauce and a fried egg to serve.

Storage

The tomato and bean sauce can be stored in an airtight container in the refrigerator for up to 3 days or the freezer for up to 3 months, then reheated.

Health Benefits

Numerous studies highlight the health attributes of onions and garlic, particularly their antibacterial, antiviral and antifungal properties. Both have been found to reduce levels of harmful LDL cholesterol and high blood pressure as well as raising beneficial HDL cholesterol, reducing the risk of heart disease and strokes.

Food Facts per Portion

Calories 296kcal • Total Carbs 31.4g • total sugar 11g • added sugar 0g

Asparagus, Courgette/Zucchini & Chive Omelette

Ⓥ Ⓞ ⊜

This open omelette, topped with spring vegetables, makes an easy light, summery lunch. Serve with a green salad and new potatoes in their skins.

SERVES 1   **PREPARATION** 10 minutes   **COOKING** 7–8 minutes

5 broad/fava bean pods

1 small courgette/zucchini, cut into ribbons with a vegetable peeler

4 asparagus spears, trimmed

1 tsp sunflower oil

2 eggs, lightly beaten

1 tbsp low-fat garlic soft cheese/farmer's cheese

1 tbsp chopped chives

salt and freshly ground black pepper

1   Shell the broad/fava beans and steam them with the courgette/zucchini and asparagus for about 4 minutes or until the vegetables are tender. Remove the tough outer skin from the beans to reveal the bright green inside.

2   Meanwhile, heat the oil in a non-stick frying pan. Season the eggs and pour them into the pan. Turn the pan until the egg mixture coats the base. Cook for 2–3 minutes, then slip the flat omelette onto a plate.

3   Place a spoonful of soft/farmer's cheese in the middle of the omelette, top with the vegetables, then sprinkle with the chives before serving.

Health Benefits

Asparagus was used as a medicine long before it was eaten as a food. Rich in vitamin C, asparagus also has diuretic and laxative properties.

Food Facts per Portion

Calories 231kcal • Total Carbs 3.7g • total sugar 2g • added sugar 0g

Mediterranean Potato Salad

This substantial salad makes a nutritious, complete meal in itself. Simply scrub the potatoes rather than peeling them, to help retain the fibre and nutrients found in or just below the skin. Fibre helps to keep blood-sugar levels steady following a meal.

SERVES 4   **PREPARATION** 15 minutes   **COOKING** 10–15 minutes

400g/14oz new potatoes, scrubbed and halved (if large)

200g/7oz/1½ cups fine green beans, trimmed and halved

1 large handful wild rocket

1 Little Gem lettuce, shredded

3 large vine-ripened tomatoes, cut into wedges

1 small red onion, thinly sliced into rings

200g/7oz tinned tuna in spring water, drained and flaked

16 small black olives

4 hard-boiled eggs

salt and freshly ground black pepper

Dressing:

4 tbsp reduced-fat mayonnaise

3 tbsp skimmed milk

1 tsp honey

4½ tsp fresh lemon juice

1   Cook the potatoes in a saucepan of boiling water for 10–15
    minutes until tender, then drain and set aside. Meanwhile,
    steam the green beans until tender and cool under cold
    running water.

2   Arrange the rocket and Little Gem lettuce on a serving platter,
    then top with the potatoes, beans, tomatoes, red onion, tuna
    and olives. Halve the eggs, arrange them on top and season.

3   Mix together the ingredients for the dressing and season.
    Drizzle over the salad and serve.

Storage

The undressed salad can be stored in an airtight container in the
refrigerator for up to 1 day. Add the dressing just before serving.

Health Benefits

Tuna loses much of its omega-3 content through the canning
process, but nevertheless it remains a good source of valuable
protein and is low in saturated fat.

Food Facts per Portion

Calories 265kcal • Total Carbs 22.8g • total sugar 8.2g • added sugar 1.6g

Pasta Puttanesca

There is no need to stick to pasta made from refined wheat when there are so many different types to choose from: buckwheat, corn and quinoa to name but a few. Spelt is used here, and although it is an ancient wheat variety, it has a lower GL (glycaemic load) than the common wheat we are familiar with.

SERVES 4   **PREPARATION** 10 minutes   **COOKING** 12 minutes

300g/10^{1}/$_{2}$oz wholegrain spelt spaghetti

2 tbsp olive oil

2 garlic cloves, finely chopped

6 tinned anchovy fillets

400g/14oz/1^{2}/$_{3}$ cups tinned cherry tomatoes

200g/7oz tinned chickpeas/garbanzo beans in water, drained and rinsed

1 tsp dried oregano

3 tbsp small black stoned olives

^{1}/$_{2}$ tsp crushed dried chillies (optional)

1 heaped tbsp small capers, drained

1 tbsp chopped parsley

salt and freshly ground black pepper

1 Cook the pasta following the instructions on the packet until al dente. Meanwhile, heat the oil in a saucepan, add the garlic and fry for 30 seconds, then add the anchovies and cook, stirring, for 2 minutes or until they begin to break up.

2   Stir in the tomatoes, chickpeas/garbanzo beans, oregano, olives, crushed chillies, if using, and capers and bring to the boil, then reduce the heat and simmer, half-covered, for 5 minutes until beginning to thicken. Stir the sauce occasionally to stop it sticking to the base of the pan

3   Drain the pasta, reserving 3 tablespoons of the cooking water. Return the pasta to the pan with the water and sauce and heat through, stirring until combined. Season to taste, then sprinkle with parsley before serving.

Storage

The pasta sauce can be stored in an airtight container in the refrigerator for 3 days, then reheated.

Health Benefits

Spelt was one of the first grains to be grown (as long ago as 2500BC) and is currently experiencing a renewal in popularity. Although part of the wheat family, spelt is generally tolerated by those people with a wheat intolerance, though it should be avoided by people with coeliac disease. It has a higher nutritional value than wheat, is richer in vitamins B and E and also contains significant amounts of protein.

Food Facts per Portion

Calories 366kcal • Total Carbs 54.9g • total sugar 5.8g • added sugar 0g

Chinese Egg & Prawn/Shrimp Rice

This simple meal is a great way of using up leftover brown rice. Brown basmati is best, since the grains remain separate yet fluffy when cooked. Do make sure you reheat the cooked rice thoroughly until it is piping hot.

SERVES 4   **PREPARATION** 20 minutes   **COOKING** 15 minutes

1 tbsp sunflower oil

1 tsp sesame oil

1 large onion, sliced

1 large red bell pepper, halved, deseeded and sliced

200g/7oz/scant 2 cups choi sum, sliced

2 large garlic cloves, chopped

5cm/2in piece fresh root ginger, peeled and grated

150g/5½oz/1¼ cups frozen petit pois

200g/7oz cooked and peeled prawns/shrimp

450g/1lb/2¼ cups cooked cold brown basmati rice

3 tbsp reduced-salt soy sauce (no added sugar)

3 eggs, lightly beaten

1 tbsp sesame seeds, toasted (optional)

1 handful coriander/cilantro leaves, chopped

freshly ground black pepper

1 Heat the sunflower and sesame oils in a large wok or frying pan. Add the onion and stir-fry for 3 minutes, then toss in the red bell pepper and choi sum and cook, stirring, for 3 minutes.

2 Next add the garlic, ginger and petits pois, then stir-fry for another minute. Stir in the prawns/shrimp and rice and heat through, stirring continuously.

3 Make a well in the centre of the rice and pour in the soy sauce and eggs and draw the rice into the egg mixture, stirring continuously, making sure it does not stick to the bottom of the wok.

4 When the egg has cooked, season with pepper, sprinkle with the sesame seeds, if using, and scatter with the coriander/cilantro before serving.

Health Benefits

The health benefits of ginger have been well documented for centuries, but more recent research has shown that ginger reduces blood pressure and boosts circulation. Ginger also increases the release of insulin secretion and increases the uptake of glucose in fat cells.

Food Facts per Portion

Calories 385kcal • Total Carbs 42.8g • total sugar 6.9g • added sugar 0g

Spiced Prawns/Shrimp on Chapatti

Mustard seeds give a warming, nutty flavour and aroma to this light, quick meal. You can use cooked instead of raw prawns/shrimp: just simply heat them through for 1–2 minutes.

SERVES 1	**PREPARATION** 10 minutes	**COOKING** 8 minutes

1 tbsp sunflower oil

1 red onion, sliced

1 tsp black mustard seeds

1 tsp cumin seeds

1/2 tsp crushed dried chillies

1 large garlic clove, chopped

1 courgette/zucchini, sliced

8 raw large king prawns/jumbo shrimp, peeled

1 tbsp fresh lemon juice

1 wholemeal chapatti, warmed

salt and freshly ground black pepper

1   Heat the oil in a wok and stir-fry the onion for 3 minutes. Add the spices and garlic and stir-fry for another minute.

2   Add the courgette/zucchini and prawns/shrimp and stir-fry for 3 minutes or until the prawns/shrimp turn pink and are cooked through. Stir in the lemon juice and season to taste.

3   Meanwhile, warm the wholemeal chapatti in a dry frying pan
    for 30 seconds on each side. Serve the spiced prawns/shrimp
    on top of the warm chapatti.

Storage

The stir-fry mixture can be stored in an airtight container in
the refrigerator for up to 2 days, then served cold as a spiced
prawn/shrimp salad.

Health Benefits

Recent data suggests that prawns/shrimp provide reasonable
amounts of omega-3 fatty acids. Like fish, prawns/shrimp are also
low in saturated fat and brimming with protein, B vitamins, zinc,
magnesium, selenium and iodine.

Food Facts per Portion

Calories 280kcal • Total Carbs 28g • total sugar 4.9g • added sugar 0g

Salmon & Onion Frittata

O

Tinned salmon makes a convenient store-cupboard standby for dishes such as fishcakes, pasta sauces, fish pies or tarts. You could also use tinned tuna or crab for this frittata. Serve with a large green salad.

SERVES 6   **PREPARATION** 10 minutes   **COOKING** 18 minutes

420g/15oz tinned wild red salmon, drained

1 tbsp sunflower oil

1 large onion, sliced

6 eggs, lightly beaten

salt and freshly ground black pepper

1   Turn the salmon out onto a plate and remove any skin and bones, then flake the fish into large chunks.

2   Heat the oil in a medium frying pan with a heatproof handle, then fry the onion for 8 minutes until softened and slightly golden. Stir in the salmon, retaining the chunks as much as possible. Spread the salmon and onion mixture over the base of the pan in an even layer.

3   Preheat the grill to medium. Season the eggs and pour them evenly into the pan. Cook for about 5 minutes over a medium-low heat until the base is light golden and set.

4 Place the pan under the preheated grill and cook the frittata
for about 3 minutes until the eggs have just set. Slide out onto
a plate and cut into wedges before serving.

Storage

Can be wrapped in kitchen foil and stored in the refrigerator for
up to 3 days.

Health Benefits

Long chain omega-3 fatty acids are found in plentiful amounts in
salmon and are essential for maintaining a healthy nervous system
as well as benefiting the brain, skin and hair.

Food Facts per Portion

Calories 209kcal • Total Carbs 3.1g • total sugar 2.2g • added sugar 0g

Chicken Tacos with Lime Guacamole

Char-grilling or griddling is a great low-fat method of cooking. Serve the tacos with a green salad and tomato salsa.

SERVES 4

PREPARATION 10 minutes, plus marinating   **COOKING** 20–25 minutes

1 tbsp fajita spice mix

¼ tsp crushed dried chillies

4 tsp olive oil, plus extra for brushing

400g/14oz lean chicken breast, cut into strips

1 large red onion, halved and sliced

1 large red bell pepper, halved, deseeded and cut into strips

2 courgettes/zucchini, cut into strips

8 corn taco shells

For the guacamole:

1 large avocado, halved, pitted and flesh scooped out

juice of 1 lime, plus a few strips of zest

1 small garlic clove, minced

salt and freshly ground black pepper

1   Mix together the fajita spice mix, crushed chillies and oil in a shallow dish. Add the chicken and turn to coat. Set aside in the refrigerator, covered, for about 1 hour to marinate.

2 To make the guacamole, put the avocado, lime juice and garlic in a bowl. Use a fork to mash the avocado to a coarse purée. Season to taste and scatter with the lime zest before serving.

3 Preheat the oven to 180°C/350°F/Gas 4. Heat a griddle pan and remove the chicken from the marinade using tongs, then griddle for 8–10 minutes, turning once, until cooked. Remove from the pan and keep warm.

4 Put the onion and pepper in the griddle pan, brushing them with a little oil. Cook for 8 minutes, turning once, until slightly blackened, then remove and keep hot with the chicken while you griddle the courgettes/zucchini for 6 minutes.

5 Meanwhile, stand the taco shells upright on a baking sheet and warm them in the oven following the packet instructions. Remove from the oven and divide the chicken and vegetables between the tacos and top with a spoonful of guacamole.

Health Benefits

Avocados may have a high fat content, but it is the heart-friendly monounsaturated type. What's more, they are good source of lutein, which protects the eyes against age-related degeneration and cataracts. They also have cholesterol-reducing properties, are a great source of vitamin E and protect against the ageing process.

Food Facts per Portion

Calories 476kcal • Total Carbs 37.8g • total sugar 4.9g • added sugar 0g

Vegetable & Chicken Ramen

Despite the long list of ingredients, this Japanese-style soup could not be easier to make, and it is light and soothing to eat.

SERVES 4   **PREPARATION** 10 minutes   **COOKING** 18–20 minutes

400g/14oz skinless, boneless chicken breasts, sliced into thin strips

olive oil, for brushing

200g/7oz wholegrain soba noodles

4 tbsp brown rice or other miso paste

2 tbsp reduced-salt soy sauce (no added sugar)

5cm/2in piece fresh root ginger, peeled and cut into thin strips

1 large carrot, peeled, halved and cut into matchsticks

6 spring onions/scallions, thinly sliced on the diagonal

1 red bell pepper, halved, deseeded and cut into thin strips

2 pak choi/bok choy, cut lengthways

1 tsp toasted sesame oil

1 tsp nori flakes

1 small handful coriander/cilantro leaves

1   Preheat the grill to high and line the grill pan with foil. Place the chicken in the grill pan and brush with oil, then grill for 5–6 minutes on each side until cooked right through.

2   Meanwhile, cook the noodles following the packet instructions, then drain and refresh under cold running water and set aside.

3   Put 1 litre/35fl oz/4 cups hot water in a saucepan, add the
    miso paste and stir until dissolved. Add the soy sauce, ginger,
    carrot, spring onions/scallions, red bell pepper and pak
    choi/bok choy and bring to the boil, then reduce the heat and
    simmer, uncovered, for about 3 minutes until the pak choi/bok
    choy is just tender.

4   Divide the noodles and chicken among four shallow bowls
    and spoon over the vegetables and bouillon. Drizzle over the
    sesame oil, then sprinkle with the nori flakes and coriander/
    cilantro leaves before serving.

Storage

Can be stored in an airtight container in the refrigerator for up to
2 days.

Health Benefits

The main component of miso is fermented soya beans, although
there are various types available that may also include rice (as used
here), barley or wheat. In some parts of China and Japan, drinking
a bowl of miso a day is a must – ensuring a long and healthy life. It
is particularly good for the digestion and is said to help to eliminate
toxins from the body.

Food Facts per Portion

Calories 423kcal • Total Carbs 42.7g • total sugar 5g • added sugar 0g

Turkey & Apple Salad

O 🥑 🌿 🍲

Try to eat a rainbow of different-coloured fruits and vegetables each day, since each colour provides different healthy phyto-chemicals (plant nutrients), vitamins and minerals.

SERVES 4   **PREPARATION** 15 minutes   **COOKING** 5 minutes

2 tsp olive oil

2 wholemeal pitta breads, split open and torn into
   bite-sized pieces

1 apple, quartered, cored and diced

juice of ½ lemon

2 Little Gem lettuces, leaves shredded

1 carrot, peeled and grated

½ small red cabbage, cored and shredded

2 celery sticks, finely sliced

300g/10½oz cooked skinless turkey breast, sliced

Dressing:

4 tbsp 0% fat Greek yogurt

3 tbsp reduced-fat mayonnaise

1 tsp extra-virgin olive oil

1 garlic clove, minced

salt and freshly ground black pepper

1   Heat the oil in a large frying pan. Add the pitta bread pieces and heat, turning occasionally, until crisp, then set aside to cool.

2   Meanwhile, toss the apple in 2 teaspoons of the lemon juice. Arrange the lettuces, carrot, cabbage, celery and apple in a serving dish.

3   Mix together the ingredients for the dressing with the remaining lemon juice and season well. Arrange the turkey on top of the salad, drizzle the dressing over the top and serve.

Storage

The undressed salad can be stored in an airtight container in the refrigerator for up to 1 day. Add the dressing just before serving.

Health Benefits

Studies show that eating cabbage more than once a week can reduce the likelihood of cancer of the colon in men by up to 65 per cent. Raw cabbage is particularly potent and has antiviral and anti-bacterial properties.

Food Facts per Portion

Calories 297kcal • Total Carbs 25.2g • total sugar 6g • added sugar 0g

Bacon, Lentil & Pepper Salad

Tinned lentils keep the preparation of this crunchy salad quick and easy. If you prefer to use dried green or Puy lentils instead, cook them in boiling water until tender.

SERVES 4   **PREPARATION** 15 minutes   **COOKING** 7–9 minutes

6 reduced-salt bacon rashers

1 large red bell pepper, halved, deseeded and diced

2 celery sticks, thinly sliced

6 spring onions/scallions, thinly sliced

400g/14oz tinned green lentils, drained and rinsed

Dressing:

2 tbsp extra-virgin olive oil

1 tbsp apple cider vinegar

1 tsp Dijon mustard

1 garlic clove, halved

salt and freshly ground black pepper

1   Preheat the grill to high and line the grill pan with foil. Cook the bacon under the preheated grill until crisp. Remove and leave to cool slightly, then snip into bite-sized pieces.

2   While the bacon is grilling, put the red bell pepper, celery, spring onions/scallions and green lentils in a serving bowl. Add the bacon to the bowl.

3   Put all the dressing ingredients in a bowl or jug and stir them together using a fork or small whisk. Set aside for 10 minutes to allow the garlic to infuse. ?Then remove before pouring??

4   Pour the dressing over the lentil salad, toss together until combined and serve.

Storage

The undressed salad can be kept in an airtight container in the refrigerator for up to 3 days. Add the dressing just before serving.

Health Benefits

Hippocrates is said to have prescribed apple cider vinegar for respiratory problems. In fact, this 'super food' has been praised for centuries for its numerous health benefits, including improving the symptoms of arthritis, joint pain, acne, candida, digestive disorders and acid reflux. It is even said to aid weight loss. Make sure you buy the unrefined organic variety.

Food Facts per Portion

Calories 211kcal • Total Carbs 12.1g • total sugar 1.8g • added sugar 0g

Beef & Broccoli Stir-Fry

Stir-frying is an excellent method of low-fat cooking. Serve this colourful stir-fry with wholegrain noodles or brown rice. Researchers have found that whole grains may help to reduce the risk of type 2 diabetes, partly attributed to the presence of magnesium, which promotes healthy blood-sugar control.

SERVES 4   PREPARATION 15 minutes   COOKING 10 minutes

350g/12oz long-stem broccoli, stalks diagonally sliced, florets separated

2 tbsp sunflower oil

400g/14oz lean beef sirloin, thinly sliced across the grain

1 yellow bell pepper, halved, deseeded and sliced

1 red bell pepper, halved, deseeded and sliced

3 large garlic cloves, sliced

5cm/2in piece fresh root ginger, peeled and cut into thin matchsticks

3 tbsp Chinese cooking wine

3 tbsp fresh orange juice

2–3 tbsp reduced-salt soy sauce (no added sugar)

1 tsp toasted sesame oil

freshly ground black pepper

1   Steam the broccoli for 2 minutes, then refresh under cold running water.

2   Heat the oil in a wok or frying pan until hot. Add half of the beef and stir-fry for 2 minutes until browned and sealed all over. Remove the beef from the wok using a slotted spoon and set aside while you cook the remaining beef.

3   Pour away all but 1 tablespoon of the oil. Put the broccoli, yellow and red bell peppers, garlic and ginger into the wok and stir-fry for 2 minutes.

4   Return the beef to the wok and stir, then pour in the Chinese cooking wine, orange juice, soy sauce and sesame oil and stir-fry for another minute. Season with pepper and serve.

Health Benefits

Red meat, such as beef, provides plentiful amounts of iron in a readily absorbable form. Iron is vital for making new red blood cells. Broccoli is a nutritional powerhouse, providing numerous vitamins and minerals and beneficial plant compounds.

Food Facts per Portion

Calories 247kcal • Total Carbs 5.2g • total sugar 4.8g • added sugar 0g

Variations

This stir-fry is incredibly versatile and it is possible to vary the choice of vegetables and meat depending on your favourite ingredients and what you have to hand. In place of the beef, try strips of chicken or turkey and stir-fry them for 6–8 minutes or until cooked through.

When it comes to vegetables, you could swap the broccoli and sweet bell peppers for pak choi/bok choy, halved lengthways and sliced onion and carrot. Asparagus, Chinese leaves, mangetout and sugar snap peas/snow peas also work well in a stir-fry

To add a finishing touch, scatter over chopped spring onions and toasted sesame seeds.

DINNERS

This diverse selection of recipes takes its inspiration from some of the cuisines of the world, including Spanish Chorizo & Bean Stew, Mexican Vegetarian Chilli in Tortilla Baskets, Thai Mussels with Noodles, Moroccan Chicken Pilaf and Beef & Lentil Curry. A nutrient-rich combination of ingredients, such as wholegrains, pulses, lentils and vegetables, features heavily within the recipes in this chapter. These also have a stabilizing influence on blood-sugar levels, keeping hunger pangs at bay for longer. Much is made of low-fat sources of protein, including chicken, seafood, beans and lean cuts of beef, which when combined with a high-fibre carbohydrate food will satisfy the appetite and provide long-term energy, helping to 'dilute' the effects that sugar has on your body and to even out unsettling peaks and troughs in blood sugar – ideally negating the desire to snack on sugary foods later on in the day!

Fresh, vibrant and packed with flavour, these healthy main meals have been created to appeal to the whole family, but ingredients can easily be halved to serve two people instead, if desired.

Ribollita

This thick Tuscan soup made with various vegetables and beans is traditionally made one-day ahead, hence the name 'ribollita", which means 're-boiled".

SERVES 4   **PREPARATION** 15 minutes   **COOKING** 35 minutes

2 tbsp olive oil

1 large onion, roughly chopped

2 leeks, sliced

2 carrots, peeled and sliced

2 celery sticks, sliced

2 large garlic cloves, chopped

2 bay leaves

2 good-sized rosemary sprigs

1.2 litres/44fl oz/5 cups low-salt vegetable bouillon

3 large vine-ripened tomatoes, quartered, deseeded and chopped

$\frac{1}{2}$ tsp crushed dried chillies

175g/6oz/1$\frac{1}{2}$ cups cavolo nero, tough stalks removed and leaves shredded

400g/14oz tinned cannellini beans in water, drained and rinsed

salt and freshly ground black pepper

4 heaped tsp black olive tapenade, to serve (optional)

1   Heat the oil in a large saucepan and sauté the onion for 5 minutes, then add the leeks, carrots, celery and garlic and cook for another 4 minutes. Add the bay leaves, rosemary, bouillon, tomatoes and crushed chillies and bring to the boil, then reduce the heat and simmer, half-covered, for 15 minutes.

2   Add the cavolo nero and beans, then cook, half-covered, for a further 10 minutes until the vegetables are tender. Remove a third of the soup and purée in a blender or food processor, then return to the pan.

3   Season the soup to taste and reheat, if necessary, then serve topped with a spoonful of tapenade, if using.

Storage

Can be stored in an airtight container in the refrigerator for up to 3 days.

Health Benefits

Cavolo nero is part of the cabbage family, and, as such, boasts an extraordinary number of health properties. The plant compounds in this group are believed to provide a potent anticarcinogenic cocktail, stimulating the body's defence system.

Food Facts per Portion

Calories 163kcal • Total Carbs 16.5g • total sugar 8g • added sugar 0g

Lemon & Spinach Lentils with Egg

Ⓥ Ⓞ ☺

Puy lentils have a great affinity with mustard, spinach and eggs and make a great, simple supper dish. Serve with crusty wholemeal bread, pitta bread or new potatoes in their skins.

SERVES 4   PREPARATION 15 minutes   COOKING 30–35 minutes

200g/7oz/1 cup Puy or green lentils, rinsed

2 bay leaves

2 tbsp olive oil

2 onions, roughly chopped

4 large/extra-large eggs

7 vine-ripened tomatoes, quartered, deseeded and cut into chunks

225g/8oz/1¹/₂ cups spinach, washed, drained well and shredded

3 heaped tsp Dijon mustard

4 tbsp reduced-fat crème fraîche

juice of 1¹/₂ lemons

salt and freshly ground black pepper

1 Cover the lentils with cold water in a saucepan, add the bay leaves and bring to the boil, then reduce the heat and simmer, half-covered, for 25–30 minutes until tender but not mushy. Drain the lentils and set aside, discarding the bay leaves.

2 Meanwhile, heat the olive oil in a sauté pan and fry the onions, covered, for 10 minutes until softened. At the same time, bring the eggs gently to the boil in a pan of water and boil for 4 minutes, then remove from the pan. Add the tomatoes and spinach to the onion mixture and cook, stirring, for another 2 minutes until the spinach has wilted.

3 Add the cooked lentils to the pan with the Dijon mustard, crème fraîche and lemon juice, stir until combined and heated through, then season to taste.

4 Spoon the lentils onto four plates. Halve the eggs and place on top of the lentils before serving.

Storage
The lentil mixture can be stored in an airtight container in the refrigerator for up to 2 days.

Health Benefits
Like other types of lentil, Puy lentils are a low-fat nutritious source of fibre, protein, folic acid and iron. Eggs are a good source of B-vitamins and choline, which have been found to aid brain function.

Food Facts per Portion
Calories 368kcal • Total Carbs 34.8g • total sugar 11.2g • added sugar 0g

Vegetarian Chilli in Tortilla Baskets

A soft, floury tortilla makes a perfect crisp basket when baked, and this can be filled with all manner of goodies – here it is a vegetarian chilli.

SERVES 4   **PREPARATION** 15 minutes   **COOKING** 40 minutes

2 tbsp olive oil, plus extra for brushing

1 large onion, finely chopped

2 tsp cumin seeds

3 large garlic cloves, chopped

1 hot red chilli, halved, deseeded and chopped

1 large red bell pepper, halved, deseeded and diced

2 courgettes/zucchini, diced

1 tsp ground coriander

½ tsp hot chilli powder

400g/14oz tinned kidney beans in water, drained and rinsed

600g/1lb 5oz/2½ cups tinned chopped tomatoes

1 tbsp tomato paste

4 large soft tortillas

4 tsp soured cream

1 small avocado, halved, pitted, peeled and diced

2 tbsp chopped coriander/cilantro leaves

salt and freshly ground black pepper

1 Heat the oil in a saucepan and sauté the onion for 8 minutes. Stir in the cumin seeds, garlic, chilli, red bell pepper and courgettes/zucchini and cook for another 5 minutes.

2 Stir in the spices, kidney beans, tomatoes and tomato paste, and bring to the boil, then reduce the heat and simmer, half-covered, for 15 minutes, stirring occasionally. Season.

3 Preheat the oven to 180°C/350°F/Gas 4. Stand four heatproof cereal bowls upside down on a baking sheet and brush the base and sides with oil. Carefully drape the tortillas over the top. Bake in the preheated oven for 8–10 minutes until crisp, then remove, leave to cool and lift the tortillas off the bowls.

4 Spoon in the chilli and top each serving with a spoonful of soured cream, some avocado and a scattering of coriander/cilantro.

Storage

The chilli can be stored in an airtight container in the refrigerator for up to 3 days, then reheated.

Health Benefits

The lycopene in tomatoes protects against heart disease, strokes and destructive free radicals in the nervous system.

Food Facts per Portion

Calories 313kcal • Total Carbs 39.4g • total sugar 11.6g • added sugar 0g

Masoor Dahl

This red lentil dahl can be served as a main dish with brown basmati rice. Despite the many ingredients, it is very easy to make.

SERVES 4   **PREPARATION** 20 minutes   **COOKING** 45 minutes

2 tbsp sunflower oil

1 large onion, finely chopped

3 large garlic cloves, chopped

4cm/1½in piece fresh root ginger, peeled and finely chopped

1 tbsp cumin seeds

2 tsp yellow mustard seeds

2 tsp ground coriander

1 tsp hot chilli powder

1 tsp turmeric

10 curry leaves

1 bay leaf

1 large carrot, peeled and diced

140g/5oz/generous ½ cup split red lentils, rinsed

600ml/21fl oz/scant 2½ cups low-salt vegetable bouillon

90ml/3fl oz/heaped ⅓ cup tinned chopped tomatoes

200ml/7fl oz/generous ¾ cup light coconut milk

2 tsp fresh lemon juice

1 handful coriander/cilantro leaves, chopped

2 tbsp toasted flaked almonds

salt and freshly ground black pepper

1 Heat half of the oil in a large heavy-based saucepan and fry the onion for 10 minutes until softened and beginning to turn golden. Add the garlic, ginger, cumin and mustard seeds and cook for 1 minute.

2 Stir in the ground spices, curry leaves, bay leaf, carrot and lentils and cook for 1 minute until coated in the spice mixture. Pour in the bouillon, chopped tomatoes and coconut milk and bring to the boil, then reduce the heat and simmer, half-covered, for 25 minutes, stirring occasionally, until the lentils are very tender.

3 Season the lentils to taste and stir in the lemon juice and half of the coriander. Serve the dahl scattered with the remaining coriander/cilantro and the flaked almonds.

Storage

Can be stored in an airtight container in the refrigerator for up to 3 days.

Health Benefits

Lentils are small nutritional powerhouses: as well as a useful, low-fat source of protein, they also provide beneficial amounts of B vitamins, zinc and iron.

Food Facts per Portion

Calories 250kcal • Total Carbs 26.8g • total sugar 7.8g • added sugar 0g

Spice-crusted Salmon with Cucumber Salad

The spice crust helps to cut the richness of the salmon and adds plenty of flavour with minimum effort. Serve the salmon with a spoonful of garlicky tzatziki (see page 20).

SERVES 4   **PREPARATION** 15 minutes   **COOKING** 6–8 minutes

1 tbsp coriander seeds

1 tbsp cumin seeds

1 tbsp yellow mustard seeds

¼ tsp crushed dried chillies

1 tsp dried thyme

4 salmon fillets, about 150g/5½oz each

1–2 tbsp olive oil

salt and freshly ground black pepper

Cucumber salad:

1 small cucumber

2 carrots, peeled

1 small red onion, thinly cut into rings

1 tbsp lime juice

2 tsp sesame seeds, toasted

1 Grind the coriander seeds, cumin seeds, mustard seeds and crushed chillies using a pestle and mortar to make a coarse powder, then stir in the thyme and seasoning. Spoon the spice mix over the top of the salmon, pressing it into the fish until you have a thick coating.

2 Heat the oil in a large non-stick frying pan and place the fish, spice-crust down, in the pan. Cook for about 6–8 minutes depending on the thickness of the fillet, turning once, until cooked but still pink in the centre.

3 Meanwhile, slice the cucumber and carrots into ribbons using a vegetable peeler. Combine the cucumber, carrots and red onion in a serving dish. Pour over the lime juice, sprinkle with sesame seeds and season to taste.

4 Serve the salmon hot with the salad, or leave until cold.

Storage

The cooked salmon can be stored in an airtight container in the refrigerator for up to 2 days.

Health Benefits

The omega-3 fatty acids found in salmon relieve depression, as they appear to enhance the effects of the brain's neurotransmitters that are responsible for mood control.

Food Facts per Portion

Calories 349kcal • Total Carbs 2.9g • total sugar 2.3g • added sugar 0g

Lemon Fish with Salsa Verde

This simply cooked dish is bursting with fresh summery flavours, including herbs and lemon. Serve with new potatoes in their skins and steamed vegetables.

SERVES 4   **PREPARATION** 15 minutes   **COOKING** 17–20 minutes

4 thick pollock fillets, about 175g/6oz each

olive oil, for brushing

8 slices of lemon

salt and freshly ground black pepper

Salsa verde:

4 tbsp olive oil

2 garlic cloves, minced

1 tbsp capers, drained and rinsed

90ml/3fl oz/heaped ⅓ cup chopped parsley

4 tbsp chopped basil

juice of 1 lemon

1 Preheat the oven to 200°C/400°F/Gas 6. Brush each pollock fillet with olive oil. Place each fillet on a piece of foil, large enough to cover the fish, and make a parcel.

2 Top each fillet with 2 slices of lemon and season. Fold over the foil to encase the fish, then bake in the preheated oven for 17–20 minutes until just cooked and opaque.

3 Meanwhile, put all the salsa verde ingredients in a blender and process until finely chopped. Season to taste.

4 Remove the parcels from the oven. Carefully unfold each parcel and place the fish on a plate. Drizzle any juices over the top and serve with a spoonful of the salsa verde.

Storage

The salsa verde can be stored in an airtight container in the refrigerator for up to 2 days.

Health Benefits

White fish, such as pollock, have a very low glycaemic index, meaning that they have relatively little impact on blood-sugar levels compared to sugary carbohydrate foods, which cause more severe swings and subsequent uneven energy levels.

Food Facts per Portion

Calories 245kcal • Total Carbs 0.8g • total sugar 0.5g • added sugar 0g

Seafood Hotpot with Rouille

O Ø Ø ⊗

This Spanish-influenced seafood stew is infused with saffron, smoked paprika and garlic. Serve with steamed green vegetables.

SERVES 4   **PREPARATION** 15 minutes   **COOKING** 35 minutes

350g/12oz baby new potatoes, scrubbed and halved, if large

2 tbsp olive oil

1 onion, finely sliced

1 red bell pepper, halved, deseeded and sliced

1 tbsp thyme leaves

2 bay leaves

1 good pinch of saffron

1 tsp smoked paprika

200ml/7fl oz/generous ¾ cup dry white wine

200g/7oz/heaped ½ cup tinned chopped tomatoes

300ml/10½fl oz/1¼ cups low-salt vegetable bouillon

400g/14oz white fish fillets, skinned and cut into bite-sized pieces

300g/10½oz mixed cooked seafood

salt and freshly ground black pepper

Rouille

1 garlic clove, minced

4 tbsp reduced-fat mayonnaise

1 tsp harissa (chilli paste)

1 Combine the rouille ingredients, season to taste and set aside.

2 Cook the potatoes in plenty of boiling water for 10–15 minutes until tender, then drain and set aside.

3 Meanwhile, heat the oil in a large saucepan and fry the onion for 8 minutes, stirring occasionally. Add the pepper, thyme, bay leaves, saffron and paprika, and cook for 3 minutes. Add the wine and bring to the boil, then cook for about 5 minutes until reduced and the alcohol is burnt off. Reduce the heat, add the tomatoes and bouillon and simmer, half-covered, for 10 minutes.

4 Add the fish and potatoes and cook for 3 minutes, then add the seafood and heat through for a couple of minutes, stirring gently. Season to taste. Serve in bowls with a spoonful of rouille.

Storage
The rouille and sauce can be stored in airtight containers in the refrigerator for up to 2 days. Heat the sauce and continue the recipe from step 4 when ready to serve.

Health Benefits
Seafood is a good source of zinc, which is a crucial mineral for the brain, immunity, fertility, synthesis of proteins and eyesight.

Food Facts per Portion
Calories 349kcal • Total Carbs 21.1g • total sugar 7.8g • added sugar 1.5g

Thai Mussels with Noodles

Full of fragrant, aromatic flavours, this Thai coconut curry with soba noodles makes a warming supper dish. Note that some brands of these noodles contain wheat.

SERVES 4   **PREPARATION** 20 minutes   **COOKING** 22 minutes

200g/7oz dried soba noodles

2 tbsp sunflower oil

6 shallots, chopped

3 large garlic cloves, chopped

2 lemongrass stalks, peeled and finely chopped

4 kaffir lime leaves

2 tbsp fish sauce

250ml/9fl oz/1 cup reduced-fat coconut milk

2 heaped tbsp Thai red curry paste, or to taste

2kg/4lb 8oz mussels, scrubbed, cleaned and thoroughly rinsed

juice of 1 lime

1 handful Thai basil leaves

1   Cook the noodles in plenty of boiling water for 3 minutes, then drain and refresh under cold running water and set aside.

2   Heat the oil in a large saucepan and cook the shallots for 5 minutes until softened. Add the garlic, lemongrass and kaffir lime leaves and cook for another minute.

3   Pour in the fish sauce, 200ml/7fl oz/generous ¾ cup water and
    the coconut milk, stir and bring to the boil, then reduce the heat,
    stir in the curry paste and simmer for 5 minutes until reduced.

4   Add the mussels (discarding any that do not shut when
    tapped), cover, and simmer over a medium heat for 5 minutes,
    shaking the pan occasionally, until the mussels have opened.
    Discard any mussels that remain closed. Stir in the lime juice.

5   Divide the noodles between four large shallow bowls, spoon
    the sauce over the top, then add the mussels. Sprinkle with
    basil before serving.

Health Benefits

Mussels are an excellent source of minerals, including the antioxidant selenium, which helps in the production of antibodies and
protects the brain from heavy metals such as mercury used in
dental fillings. Mussels also provide beneficial amounts of vitamin
B12, which is vital for the formation of red blood cells, iron,
manganese, phosphorus and zinc – an important immune booster.

Food Facts per Portion

Calories 617kcal • Total Carbs 51.6g • total sugar 5.3g • added sugar 0g

Lemon & Prawn/Shrimp Linguine

This light, summery pasta dish is full of fresh flavours and requires little in the way of preparation. You could also try replacing the prawns with flakes of cooked salmon.

SERVES 4   **PREPARATION** 10 minutes   **COOKING** 15 minutes

350g/12oz wholegrain spelt linguine

3 courgettes/zucchini, diagonally sliced

200g/7oz/scant 2 cups frozen petits pois

2 tbsp olive oil

2 large garlic cloves, finely chopped

350g/12oz cooked and peeled king prawns/jumbo shrimp

finely grated zest of 1 unwaxed lemon

3 tbsp fresh lemon juice

4 tbsp reduced-fat crème fraîche

1 small handful basil leaves

salt and freshly ground black pepper

1 Cook the pasta in boiling salted water for about 12 minutes until al dente. Drain the pasta, reserving 4 tablespoons of the cooking water.

2 Meanwhile, lightly steam the courgettes/zucchini and petits pois until just cooked.

3 While the pasta and vegetables are cooking, heat the olive oil in a heavy-based saucepan and fry the garlic over a medium-low heat for 1 minute. Add the prawns/shrimp, lemon zest and juice, crème fraiche and reserved water and cook, stirring, for about 1 minute until the prawns/shrimp are heated through.

4 Add the pasta, courgettes/zucchini and petits pois, then toss until the ingredients are combined and warmed through. Season to taste and serve sprinkled with basil leaves.

Health Benefits

Little nuggets of goodness, peas have a high nutritional value when compared to their size, providing useful amounts of vitamin C, iron and vitamin K. Heart-protecting folic acid and vitamin B6 are also found in beneficial amounts.

Food Facts per Portion

Calories 486kcal • Total Carbs 59.9g • total sugar 5.7g• added sugar 0g

Seared Tuna with Rocket & Tomatoes

This healthy warm salad provides a perfect combination of protein, carbohydrates and beneficial omega-3 fatty acids. Serve the salad with new potatoes in their skin, if liked.

SERVES 4   **PREPARATION** 15 minutes   **COOKING** 10 minutes

3 tbsp extra-virgin olive oil

3 tbsp balsamic vinegar

4 thick tuna steaks, about 175g/6oz each

8 vine-ripened tomatoes, halved, deseeded and cut into chunks

200g/7oz tinned chickpeas/garbanzo beans in water,
   drained and rinsed

2 large handfuls rocket leaves

juice of ½ lemon

salt and freshly ground black pepper

1 Mix together the olive oil and balsamic vinegar and brush a little over the tuna steaks, then season.

2 Heat a griddle pan until very hot. Griddle 2 tuna steaks at a time for about 2 minutes on each side until slightly charred on the outside but still pink in the middle. Cut the tuna into thick slices.

3 Arrange the tomatoes, chickpeas/garbanzo beans and rocket on each plate and top with the tuna. Squeeze over the lemon juice, then drizzle with the remaining olive oil and balsamic dressing. Season to taste, then serve.

Storage

The salad and dressing can be stored separately in airtight containers in the refrigerator for up to 1 day. Dress the salad just before serving.

Health Benefits

Try to include one portion of oily fish, such as tuna, once a week, since the protective effects continue to improve with regular consumption. Fresh tuna is richer in omega-3 fatty acids than tinned.

Food Facts per Portion

Calories 390kcal • Total Carbs 11.2g • total sugar 5.8g • added sugar 0g

Moroccan Chicken Pilaf

You will find ras el hanout, a traditional North African herb and spice mix, in Middle Eastern shops or in some supermarkets. Try cooking the rice in vegetable bouillon to give it extra flavour, and serve the dish with steamed green beans.

SERVES 4   **PREPARATION** 15 minutes   **COOKING** 20 minutes

2 tbsp olive oil

500g/1lb 2oz skinless, boneless chicken breasts,
   cut into bite-sized pieces

1 large onion, finely chopped

3 large garlic cloves, chopped

2 tsp cumin seeds

2 bay leaves

5cm/2in piece fresh root ginger, peeled and finely chopped

2 courgettes/zucchini, diced

1 tbsp ras el hanout spice mix

200g/7oz tinned chickpeas/garbanzo beans in water,
   drained and rinsed

375g/13oz/2 cups cold cooked brown basmati rice

2 nectarines, pitted and diced

juice of 1 lime

1 small handful coriander/cilantro leaves, roughly chopped

1 small handful mint leaves, roughly chopped

salt and freshly ground black pepper

1   Heat the oil in a large wok or frying pan. Stir-fry the chicken
    for 6 minutes until golden all over, then remove from the wok
    and keep warm.

2   Add the onion and stir-fry for 7 minutes. Next, add the garlic,
    cumin seeds, bay leaves and ginger and stir-fry for another
    minute. Add the courgettes/zucchini, ras el hanout and
    chickpeas/garbanzo beans, then stir-fry for 2 minutes.

3   Add the cooked rice, chicken, nectarines, lime juice and herbs
    and stir well as the mixture heats through. Season to taste,
    then serve.

Health Benefits

Ras el hanout is typically made up of cardamom, cinnamon, cumin,
chilli, coriander, nutmeg, mace, cloves, peppercorns and turmeric.
Spices are renowned for their digestive and carmitive properties,
helping to relieve indigestion and nausea. Many also have antibacterial qualities.

Food Facts per Portion

Calories 484kcal • Total Carbs 48.3g • total sugar 9.1g • added sugar 0g

Ginger Chicken Parcels

Cooking foods in a parcel, whether it be foil or baking parchment, helps to retain nutrients and keep moisture in. Here, the chicken is wonderfully succulent and infused with oriental flavours.

SERVES 4

PREPARATION 15 minutes, plus marinating   **COOKING** 15–20 minutes

3 tbsp reduced-salt soy sauce (no added sugar)

1 tbsp toasted sesame oil

1 hot red chilli, halved, deseeded and thinly sliced into rings (optional)

3 tbsp lime juice

625g/1lb 6oz skinless, boneless chicken breasts, cut into 2.5cm/1in-wide strips

5cm/2in piece fresh root ginger, peeled and cut into matchsticks

4 garlic cloves, thinly sliced

6 spring onions/scallions, diagonally sliced

1 large red bell pepper, halved, deseeded and thinly sliced

1 large carrot, peeled and cut into fine strips

1 tbsp toasted sesame seeds

1   Mix together the soy sauce, sesame oil, chilli, if using, and lime juice in a large shallow dish. Add the chicken and turn until coated in the marinade. Cover the dish and leave to marinate in the refrigerator for at least 1 hour or overnight.

2 Preheat the oven to 200°C/400°F/Gas 6. Using tongs, divide the chicken among 4 pieces of foil, each one large enough to make a parcel. Top the chicken with the ginger, garlic, spring onions/scallions, red bell pepper and carrot. Spoon the marinade over the top and fold up the foil to make 4 parcels.

3 Place the parcels on a large baking tray and cook in the preheated oven for 15–20 minutes until the chicken is cooked through. Remove from the oven and carefully open the parcels and place on plates. Sprinkle with the sesame seeds before serving.

Health Benefits
Chicken is rated as a good low-fat source of protein as well as selenium and vitamin B3 (niacin). Research shows that regular consumption of niacin-rich foods such as chicken could provide protection against Alzheimer's disease as well as age-related cognitive decline.

Food Facts per Portion
Calories 299kcal • Total Carbs 3.8g • total sugar 3.3g • added sugar 0g

Chicken with Gazpacho Salsa

Char-grilling is an excellent low-fat method of cooking and gives food a distinctive smoky barbecue flavour.

SERVES 4   **PREPARATION** 15 minutes   **COOKING** 25 minutes

4 skinless, boneless chicken breasts, about 175g/6oz each

olive oil, for brushing

2 tsp paprika

Gazpacho salsa:

1 yellow bell pepper, halved, deseeded and cut into small chunks

1 small red onion, thinly sliced into rings

1 small cucumber, cut lengthways into quarters, deseeded and cut into small chunks

3 large vine-ripened tomatoes, quartered, deseeded and cut into small chunks

20 pitted black olives, halved

4 tbsp chopped flat leaf parsley

juice of $\frac{1}{2}$ lemon

1 tbsp extra virgin olive oil

salt and freshly ground black pepper

1 Brush the chicken with olive oil, then sprinkle the paprika over each side.

2 Heat a griddle pan until hot. Reduce the heat to medium and griddle the chicken, 2 breasts at a time, for about 6 minutes on each side or until cooked right through. Keep warm while you cook the remaining chicken.

3 Meanwhile, put the yellow bell pepper, red onion, cucumber, tomatoes, olives and parsley in a serving bowl. Pour over the lemon juice and oil, season well and stir until combined.

4 Serve the chicken with the gazpacho salsa by the side.

Storage

The gazpacho salsa can be made 1 day in advance and stored in an airtight container in the refrigerator.

Health Benefits

Try to eat a range of different coloured vegetables (and fruit) each day to benefit from their range of nutritional attributes. One of the main benefits is that they all contain soluble fibre, which helps to stabilize blood-sugar and blood-cholesterol levels.

Food Facts per Portion

Calories 345kcal • Total Carbs 6.1g • total sugar 4.8g • added sugar 0g

Polpettine in Tomato Sauce

It's extremely quick and easy to make your own meatballs, and the same mixture can be used to make burgers – all without any unwanted additives. You could also swap the turkey mince for chicken, beef or lamb. Serve with wholemeal pasta or rice.

SERVES 4

PREPARATION 20 minutes, plus chilling   **COOKING** 20 minutes

400g/14oz lean turkey mince

55g/2oz/1 cup fresh wholemeal breadcrumbs

1 tsp dried thyme

1 egg, lightly beaten

salt and freshly ground black pepper

Tomato sauce:

2 tbsp olive oil

3 large garlic cloves, chopped

800g/1lb 12oz/3⅓ cups tinned chopped tomatoes

1 tbsp tomato paste

2 tsp dried oregano

1   To make the polpettine, mix together the turkey mince, breadcrumbs, thyme, egg and seasoning in a mixing bowl. Form the mixture into 20 walnut-sized balls, then cover and set aside for 30 minutes in the refrigerator to firm up.

2 To make the tomato sauce, heat the oil in a large sauté pan.
Fry the garlic for 1 minute, stirring, then add the chopped
tomatoes, tomato paste, oregano and seasoning. Bring up to
boiling point, then reduce the heat to a simmer.

3 Carefully add the polpettine to the pan and spoon the sauce
over to make sure the balls are covered. Simmer, half-covered,
for about 15 minutes until the polpettine are cooked and the
sauce reduced, carefully stirring the sauce to prevent it
sticking to the bottom of the pan. Serve hot.

Storage

The polpettine and tomato sauce can both be stored separately in
airtight containers in the refrigerator for 1 day.

Health Benefits

Turkey, like chicken, is a popular low-fat source of protein, but it
is only low-fat without the skin. Along with folic acid, turkey
provides a range of B vitamins, a combination that has been found
to prevent artherosclerosis.

Food Facts per Portion

Calories 331kcal • Total Carbs 16.9g • total sugar 6.5g • added sugar 0g

Beef & Lentil Curry

This classic rich curry can also be made with lamb. Serve with brown basmati rice and a cucumber and onion salad.

SERVES 4 **PREPARATION** 15 minutes **COOKING** 65 minutes

2 tbsp groundnut oil

500g/1lb 2oz lean beef brisket, cut into large bite-sized pieces

2 onions, thinly sliced

3 garlic cloves, chopped

5cm/2in piece fresh root ginger, peeled and grated

4 green cardamom pods, split

2 bay leaves

4 heaped tbsp rogan josh curry paste

200g/7oz/heaped ½ cup tinned chopped tomatoes

6 heaped tbsp tinned green lentils, drained and rinsed

125ml/4fl oz/½ cup natural low-fat bio yogurt

2 tsp fresh lemon juice

1 red chilli, halved, deseeded and sliced (optional)

salt and freshly ground black pepper

1 Heat half of the oil in a large heavy-based saucepan and brown the beef for about 2–3 minutes until the meat is sealed all over, then remove from the pan. You may have to cook the beef in 2 batches. Set the beef aside.

2   If the pan is dry, add the remaining oil (if not, then the extra oil is not needed), then sauté the onions for 8 minutes until softened and golden. Stir in the garlic, ginger, cardamom and bay leaves and cook for 1 minute, then add the curry paste.

3   Pour in 625ml/21fl oz/2½ cups water and the tinned tomatoes, stir and bring to the boil, then reduce the heat, return the beef to the pan and simmer, half-covered, for 45 minutes until the beef is tender.

4   Stir in the lentils, yogurt and lemon juice and cook until heated through. Season to taste, scatter red chilli over the top, if using, then serve.

Storage

Can be stored in an airtight container in the refrigerator for up to 3 days.

Health Benefits

Lean beef can play a part in a healthy diet if eaten in moderation. It is an excellent source of iron, zinc and B vitamins in a readily absorbable form. A lack of iron has been linked with low-energy levels, poor concentration, anaemia and learning difficulties.

Food Facts per Portion

Calories 376kcal • Total Carbs 20g • total sugar 8.4g • added sugar 0g

Spiced Beef Kebabs

These kebabs can be grilled or cooked on the barbecue for a wonderful smoky flavour. Serve the kebabs and the tahini dip with brown rice sprinkled with toasted sesame seeds.

SERVES 4

PREPARATION 15 minutes, plus marinating   **COOKING** 6 minutes

550g/1lb 4oz lean beef fillet

2 tbsp reduced-salt soy sauce (no added sugar)

1 tbsp sesame oil

1 tbsp olive oil

juice of 1 lime

2.5cm/1in piece fresh root ginger, peeled and grated

1 large garlic clove, minced

$1/2$ tsp crushed dried chillies

salt and freshly ground black pepper

Tahini dip:

125ml/4fl oz/$^1/_2$ cup natural low-fat bio yogurt

2 tbsp light tahini

1 garlic clove, minced

1 medium-hot red chilli, halved, deseeded and finely chopped

1 Flatten the beef with the end of a rolling pin, then cut into 2cm/¾in strips. Mix together the soy sauce, sesame oil, olive oil, lime juice, ginger, garlic and crushed chillies in a large shallow dish. Season well, then add the beef and turn the meat in your hands until it is coated in the marinade. Leave to marinate for at least 1 hour or overnight.

2 While the beef is marinating, make the tahini dip. Mix together the yogurt, tahini, garlic and chilli with 1 tablespoon warm water, then set aside. Preheat the grill to high.

3 Thread the beef onto 12 skewers (presoaked in water if wooden/bamboo) and cook under the preheated grill for 3 minutes, then turn the kebabs, spoon over the remaining marinade and cook for another 3 minutes.

4 Serve the kebabs with the tahini dip.

Health Benefits

Tahini, a paste made from crushed sesame seeds, is a nutritional powerhouse as well as great brain food, being high in vitamins E, B-complex, biotin and choline. It is also rich in protein and calcium, and is reputed to be a better source of these than dairy foods.

Food Facts per Portion

Calories 437kcal • Total Carbs 3.4g • total sugar 3g • added sugar 0g

Ham & Barley Broth

This sustaining and nurturing broth makes a nutritious meal.
It is a complete meal in itself, but you could also serve it with a
slice of bread and cheese if you are feeling particularly hungry.

SERVES 4   **PREPARATION** 15 minutes   **COOKING** 45 minutes

100g/3¹/₂oz/¹/₂ cup pearl barley, rinsed

1 tbsp olive oil

2 onions, sliced

2 celery sticks, sliced

2 large carrots, peeled, halved lengthways and sliced

2 turnips, peeled and cubed

1.2 litres/44fl oz/5 cups low-salt vegetable or chicken bouillon

2 bay leaves

1 bouquet garni

2 rosemary sprigs

1 sweet potato, peeled and cut into bite-sized chunks

200g/7oz thickly cut cooked reduced-salt ham, diced

salt and freshly ground black pepper

1 Put the pearl barley in a saucepan, cover with water and bring
to the boil, then reduce the heat and simmer, covered, for
25 minutes until the pearl barley is soft but not quite cooked.

2   Meanwhile, heat the oil in a large saucepan and sauté the
    onions, half-covered, for 5 minutes, then add the celery, carrots
    and turnips. Sauté the vegetables for 5 minutes, then add the
    bouillon, bay leaves, bouquet garni and rosemary. Bring to the
    boil, then reduce the heat and simmer for 10 minutes.

3   Drain the pearl barley and add it to the broth with the sweet
    potato and ham. Simmer, half-covered, for a further 20 minutes
    until the sweet potato is tender.

4   Season to taste and remove the bay leaves, bouquet garni
    and rosemary before serving.

Storage

Can be stored in an airtight container in the refrigerator for up to
3 days.

Health Benefits

Pearl barley is a much under-rated grain that provides many
nutritional benefits. Alongside cholesterol-lowering fibre, barley
provides vitamin B3 (niacin), which has been found to protect
against atherosclerosis, the furring up of the arteries.

Food Facts per Portion

Calories 302kcal • Total Carbs 37.7g • total sugar 9.2g • added sugar 0g

Spanish Chorizo & Bean Stew

A great supper for those who don't have much time on their hands and are looking for a meal that is warming and nutritious. Serve with green vegetables and crusty bread for mopping up the sauce.

SERVES 4   **PREPARATION** 10 minutes   **COOKING** 25 minutes

1 tbsp olive oil

1 large onion, chopped

250g/9oz chorizo, cut into bite-sized chunks

2 large garlic cloves, chopped

2 tsp dried thyme

400g/14oz/1²/₃ cups tinned chopped tomatoes

400g/14oz/1²/₃ cups tinned low-sugar and salt baked beans

2 tsp tomato paste

1 tsp smoked paprika

salt and freshly ground black pepper

1   Heat the oil in a large saucepan. Add the onion and fry, stirring, for 7 minutes, then add the chorizo and cook for another 3 minutes. Stir in the garlic and fry for another minute.

2   Add the thyme, tinned tomatoes and beans, tomato paste, paprika and 90ml/3fl oz/generous ¹/₃ cup water and bring to the boil, stirring occasionally. Reduce the heat and simmer, half-covered, for 10 minutes until the sauce has thickened slightly.

3 Season the stew to taste, then serve in shallow bowls.

Storage
Can be stored in an airtight container in the refrigerator for up to 3 days.

Health Benefits
Although the antiviral, antifungal and antibacterial properties of garlic are most potent when raw, cooking does not inhibit its cancer-protecting, blood-thinning and decongestant properties.

Food Facts per Portion
Calories 314kcal • Total Carbs 20.3g • total sugar 9.8g • added sugar 2.4g

Marinated Lamb with Chickpea Mash

Chickpeas/garbanzo beans make an excellent alternative to potatoes when mashed, especially when infused with garlic, herbs and the North African spice paste, harissa. The spiced lamb is delicious served simply with steamed vegetables such as green beans and broccoli.

SERVES 4

PREPARATION 15 minutes, plus marinating   COOKING 10–12 minutes

2 tbsp olive oil

1 tsp paprika

1 tsp dried thyme

1 tsp sumac

4 lean lamb steaks, about 150g/5¹/₂oz each

salt and freshly ground black pepper

Chickpea mash:

2 tbsp olive oil

3 garlic cloves, minced

1 tsp harissa

400g/14oz tinned chickpeas/garbanzo beans in water, drained and rinsed

5 tbsp semi-skimmed milk

1 handful coriander/cilantro leaves, chopped

1   Mix together the olive oil, paprika, thyme, sumac and salt and pepper in a large shallow dish. Add the lamb and turn to coat the meat in the marinade, then set aside to marinate for 1 hour.

2   Heat a griddle pan until very hot. Remove the lamb from the marinade and griddle for 6–8 minutes or until cooked to taste, turning halfway and brushing with the remaining marinade.

3   Meanwhile, to make the chickpea mash, heat the oil in a saucepan and gently fry the garlic for 1 minute, then add the harissa and chickpeas/garbanzo beans and cook for 3 minutes. Stir in the milk to warm through, then transfer everything to a blender or food processor. Purée until smooth and season to taste, then stir in three-quarters of the coriander/cilantro.

4   Divide the chickpea mash among four plates and top with the lamb. Scatter with the reserved coriander/cilantro before serving.

Storage

The chickpea mash can be stored in an airtight container in the refrigerator for up to 3 days. Reheat when ready to serve.

Health Benefits

The chickpea mash has a lower GI and GL level than mashed potato, meaning that is does not cause such large fluctuations in blood-sugar levels.

Food Facts per Portion

Calories 494kcal • Total Carbs 12.4g • total sugar 1.4g • added sugar 0g

Variation

Other canned pulses can be used in place of the chickpeas/ garbanzo beans when making the mash: you could try cannellini or haricot beans. Prepare them in the same way as the chickpeas/ garbanzo beans.

Sumac is a spice that is readily found in Middle Eastern food shops but if you find it difficult to buy, the spicy marinade can be varied according to what you have to hand and personal preference. For a more Mediterranean feel, try a combination of olive oil, 1 tsp dried oregano, 1 tsp dried thyme and ½ tsp smoked paprika. Alternatively, try a combination of olive oil and 1 tsp ground cumin, 1 tsp ground coriander, 1 tsp mild chilli powder and a good squeeze of lemon juice.

DESSERTS

Raspberry Cream Roulade, Black Forest Strudel and Baked Chocolate Bananas are just a taster of the recipes in this chapter. It doesn't seem possible that these are all low in sugar, but many are also low in fat too.

Without putting a damper on things, if following a low-sugar diet you should try to avoid eating dessert every day, but the good news is that there are numerous naturally sweet foods and alternative flavourings that will help you to create mouthwatering desserts without overloading on sugar or fat.

Importantly, there's no need to resort to artificial sweeteners, with their reported adverse effects on health. Most of the recipes rely on fresh fruit for their natural sweetness as well as natural sweeteners such as agave syrup.

There is a wide range of desserts to choose from to suit all manner of eating occasion and season, from a summery zingy Orange & Pineapple Granita to Apple Amaretti Crumbles – perfect comfort food. If time is short, the Superfood Mix, a healthy combination of nuts, berries, raw chocolate and shredded coconut, can almost literally be thrown together in a matter of minutes, and just a handful satisfies a desire for something sweet.

Superfood Mix

On occasion you may not feel like a full-blown dessert, so this combination of 'superfoods", including raw chocolate, seeds, nuts and berries, will satisfy any desire for a little sweetness. It also makes a great snack.

SERVES 4   **PREPARATION** 5 minutes   **COOKING** 3–5 minutes

2 tbsp sunflower seeds

4 tbsp flaked almonds

55g/2oz/scant ¹/₂ cup raw cacao nibs

55g/2oz/¹/₂ cup goji berries

55g/2oz/scant ¹/₂ cup unsweetened desiccated or shredded coconut

1   Toast the sunflower seeds and almonds in a dry frying pan, turning them occasionally, for 3–5 minutes or until starting to turn golden, then leave to cool.

2   Put the sunflower seeds and almonds in a bowl with the cacao nibs, goji berries and coconut, then mix until combined.

Storage

Can be stored in an airtight container for up to 1 week.

Health Benefits

Hailed as the 'food of the gods", raw cacao has received consider-able attention recently as it has been found to be one of the richest sources of antioxidants, exceeding that of red wine and green tea. Raw cacao does not contain any sugar and is rich in minerals, including sulphur – which is known as the 'beauty mineral' because of its benefits to the skin. Sulphur has long been recognised for its healing properties, helping to tone and repair the skin, hair and nails.

Food Facts per Portion

Calories 295kcal • Total Carbs 19.5g • total sugar 1.2g • added sugar 0g

Variation

Try swapping the almonds for cashew nuts or hazelnuts. Chopped apricots, raisins or dried cherries make delicious alternatives to the goji berries.

Fig, Nut & Orange Balls

Ⓥ 🄾 🄴 🄾

Packed with energy-giving dried fruit and nutritious nuts and seeds, these coconut-coated balls make an excellent and unusual dessert or snack. For Christmas, why not add a splash of brandy to the fruit mixture? Replace 1 tablespoon of the orange juice with the liqueur.

MAKES about 16   **PREPARATION** 20 minutes   **COOKING** 5 minutes

50g/1¾oz/½ cup hazelnuts, roughly chopped

50g/1¾oz/½ cup whole oats

2 tbsp sunflower seeds

2 tbsp pumpkin seeds

70g/2½oz/½ cup raisins

150g/5½oz/scant 1 cup ready-to-eat dried figs, cut into small pieces

4 tbsp fresh orange juice (not from concentrate)

unsweetened desiccated coconut, for coating

1 Put the hazelnuts and oats in a dry frying pan and toast over a medium heat, turning them frequently, for 5 minutes or until they start to turn golden and the oats become slightly crisp. Leave to cool.

2 Put the nuts, oats and seeds in a food processor or blender and process until finely chopped. Tip the mixture into a mixing bowl.

3 Put the raisins, figs and orange juice into the food processor or blender and purée until the mixture becomes a smooth, thick purée. Scrape the fruit purée into the bowl with the nut mixture and mix until combined. Cover the bowl and chill the mixture for 1 hour.

4 To make the balls, scoop up a portion of the fruit and nut mixture - about the size of a walnut – in a spoon and roll into a ball. Sprinkle the desiccated coconut on a plate and roll the ball in it until well coated. Repeat with the remaining mixture to make about 16 balls.

Storage

Can be stored in an airtight container for up to 1 week

Health Benefits

Dried figs are renowned for their fibre content, helping to relieve constipation and keep the digestive system in good working order. Rich in minerals, figs are a good source of iron, phosphorus and manganese.

Food Facts per Ball

Calories 88kcal • Total Carbs 10.1g • total sugar 8.1g • added sugar 0g

Sweet Popcorn

Shop-bought sweet popcorn tends to be loaded with sugar. This low-sugar version uses agave syrup (the sap of a Mexican cactus) as a sweetener. It is low GI and you need to use only a small amount since it is much sweeter than refined sugar.

SERVES 4   **PREPARATION** 5 minutes   **COOKING** 10 minutes

1 tbsp sesame seeds

2 tsp sunflower oil

100g/3¹/₂oz/scant 1 cup popping corn

1 tbsp agave syrup

1   Put the sesame seeds in a dry frying pan and toast over a medium-low heat, shaking the pan occasionally until the seeds are light golden. Take care because the seeds can burn easily. Set aside.

2   Put the oil in a medium saucepan with a tight-fitting lid. Add the corn in an even layer, cover with the lid and heat until the corn starts to pop. Shake the pan occasionally and continue to cook until there is no sound of popping.

3   Tip the popcorn into a bowl and spoon the agave syrup over. Sprinkle with the sesame seeds and turn the popcorn until it is coated in the syrup and seeds, then serve.

Storage

Can be stored in an airtight container for up to 1 day.

Health Benefits

Corn provides a good range of nutrients, from B vitamins, vitamins C and E, folic acid, fibre, essential fatty acids and the minerals magnesium and phosphorus. The B vitamins are essential for a healthy nervous system, energy metabolism and brain function.

Food Facts per Portion

Calories 195Kcal • Total Carbs 14.3g • total sugar 3g • added sugar 2.7g

Variation

Agave syrup is now available in many large supermarkets and health food shops, but if you have trouble finding it you could use honey or maple syrup instead.

Banana & Mango Yogurt Ice

Ⓥ ⊜ ⊛

This pure-fruit frozen yogurt contains a small amount of agave syrup to sweeten it. Serve it with a fresh mango sauce, if liked.

SERVES 8   **PREPARATION** 15 minutes, plus freezing

1 large ripe mango

2 ripe bananas, cut into chunks

500g/1lb 2oz 2% fat Greek yogurt

$\frac{1}{2}$ tsp vanilla extract

4 tbsp agave syrup

squeeze of fresh lemon juice

Mango sauce (optional):

1 ripe mango

1   Using a vegetable peeler, remove the skin from the mango, then slice the flesh away from the large central stone. Put the mango flesh and bananas in a blender or food processor with the yogurt, vanilla extract, agave syrup and lemon juice. Blend until the fruit is puréed and the mixture is thick and creamy.

2   Pour the mixture into an ice-cream maker and churn following the manufacturer's instructions. Alternatively, pour it into a shallow, lidded, freezer-proof container and freeze. Whisk or stir briskly with a fork every 2 hours to break up any ice crystals that have formed until the yogurt ice is frozen. This will help to give it a creamy texture.

3   Remove the yogurt ice from the freezer 30 minutes before
    eating to allow it to soften.

4   To make the mango sauce, if using, prepare the mango as for
    the yogurt ice, then purée the mango flesh in a blender or
    food processor until smooth. Serve the yogurt ice in scoops
    with the mango sauce spooned over the top.

Storage

The yogurt ice can be stored in an airtight freezer-proof container
in the freezer for up to 3 months.

Health Benefits

Mango contains an abundance of beta-carotene, vitamin C and
other beneficial antioxidants, which work in tandem to boost the
immune system and protect the body against free-radical damage.

Food Facts per Portion

Calories 86kcal • Total Carbs 13.4g • total sugar 10.4g •added sugar 5.5g

Orange & Pineapple Granita

Refreshing and invigorating, this zingy granita is brimming with fruity goodness. Make sure you use a ripe, juicy pineapple for the best flavour.

SERVES 4 **PREPARATION** 15 minutes, plus freezing

1 ripe pineapple, peeled, cored and cubed

juice of 4 oranges and fine strips of zest from 1 orange

2 tbsp fresh lemon juice

1 Finely chop the pineapple in a food processor or blender, then transfer to a mixing bowl. Add the orange and lemon juices and stir well.

2 Tip the mixture into a shallow, lidded, freezer-proof container and freeze for 40 minutes, then remove from the freezer and beat with a wooden spoon.

3 Repeat this process at 40-minute intervals over a 4-hour period to break the ice crystals down.

4 Spoon the granita into four glasses and sprinkle with the orange zest before serving.

Storage

Can be stored in an airtight freezer-proof container in the freezer for up to 3 months.

Health Benefits

Citrus fruit, including oranges, are brimming with vitamin C and other antioxidants. As well as helping to nurture the immune system and build new body tissues, vitamin C boosts the body's absorption of iron from non-meat sources.

Food Facts per Portion

Calories 101kcal • Total Carbs 22.7g • total sugar 22.7g • added sugar 0g

Cappuccino Pots

Ⓥ Ⓞ Ⓙ Ⓖ 🝙 Ⓥ

This is a low-fat, low-sugar version of the popular Italian dessert, tiramisu. You could also add a layer of your favourite fruit to the dessert: bananas, raspberries, strawberries or cherries work well.

SERVES 4   **PREPARATION** 15 minutes, plus cooling

---

8 sponge fingers/ladyfingers

300ml/10½fl oz/1¼ cups cold, strong black coffee

350ml/12fl oz/scant 1½ cups 2% fat Greek yogurt

½ tsp vanilla extract

2 tbsp agave syrup

8 tbsp quark

25g/1oz plain chocolate (70% cocoa solids), finely grated

1 Dip 2 of the sponge fingers into the cold coffee, making sure they do not go too soggy. Break them in half and place in the bottom of a 200ml/7fl oz/generous ¾ cup ramekin, glass or sundae dish. Repeat with the remaining biscuits and three more ramekins.

2 Whisk together the yogurt, vanilla extract, agave syrup and quark, then spoon a quarter of the creamy mixture over each layer of sponge fingers/ladyfingers. Sprinkle a quarter of the chocolate over the top of each one. Serve soon after making.

Storage

Can be covered and stored in the refrigerator for up to 1 day.

Health Benefits

Medical opinion on coffee appears to be changing. Moderate intake of coffee has been linked to a reduced risk of diabetes mellitus, heart disease, cirrhosis of the liver, gallstones, Alzheimer's and Parkinson's disease, and may help to improve memory and cognitive performance.

Food Facts per Portion

Calories 322kcal · Total Carbs 33.6g · total sugar 21.9g · added sugar 5.5g

Raspberry Yogurt Creams

Ⓥ Ⓞ Ⓞ Ⓞ Ⓞ Ⓞ

Yummy creamy, custardy fruit pots: this simple dessert ticks all the right boxes if you are looking for something sweet – but not too sweet!

SERVES 4   **PREPARATION** 10 minutes   **COOKING** 12–14 minutes

2 tbsp flaked almonds

2 tbsp sunflower seeds

2 egg yolks

250ml/9fl oz/1 cup low-fat, thick natural bio yogurt

1½ tsp vanilla extract

4 tsp fructose

150g/5½oz/scant 1 cup raspberries

1 Lightly toast the almonds and sunflower seeds in a dry frying pan until light golden, then set aside.

2 Put the egg yolks, yogurt, vanilla extract and fructose in a medium, heavy-based saucepan and heat gently, stirring frequently, until the mixture starts to bubble. Reduce the heat slightly and continue to stir for about 10–12 minutes until the mixture thickens to the consistency of custard.

3 Divide the raspberries into four ramekins. Spoon the custard over the top and serve sprinkled with the almonds and sunflower seeds.

Storage

The raspberries and custard can be covered and stored in the refrigerator for 2 days. Add the nuts and seeds just before serving.

Health Benefits

The humble almond has numerous health attributes: it is rich in monounsaturated fats, vitamin E and antioxidants. These combine to reduce harmful LDL cholesterol in the body and raise beneficial HDL cholesterol, which helps to reduce the risk of heart disease and strokes.

Food Facts per Portion

Calories 195kcal • Total Carbs 11.8g • total sugar 10.2g • added sugar 3.5g

Citrus & Pomegranate Salad with Mint

This fresh fruit salad makes a refreshing, invigorating dessert, especially after a spicy meal. If you can find red or 'blood' oranges all the better because they help to improve glucose tolerance in the body.

SERVES 4   **PREPARATION** 15 minutes

2 oranges, preferably red or 'blood"

1 red grapefruit

1 ripe pomegranate

1 handful mint leaves, roughly chopped

1   Slice off the skin of the oranges and remove any remaining pith. Thinly slice the oranges into rounds and put them – and any juice – in a serving bowl.

2   Slice off the skin of the grapefruit and remove any pith. Halve the grapefruit crossways and cut into segments. Add to the bowl with any juices.

3   Quarter the pomegranate and remove the arils (seeds). Add to the bowl with any juices. Sprinkle the mint over the fruit just before serving.

Storage

Can be covered and stored in the refrigerator for up to 1 day. Add the mint just before serving.

Health Benefits

Pomegranates are rich in antioxidants, particularly polyphenols, and negate the effect of harmful free radicals. Research shows that the fruit can promote good cardiovascular health and boost the circulatory system. It may reduce the risk of breast cancer as well as lower blood pressure if it is eaten (or the juice drunk) on a daily basis.

Food Facts per Portion

Calories 50kcal • Total Carbs 10.8g • total sugar 10.8g • added sugar 0g

Mango & Passion Fruit Fool

Transport yourself to the Tropics with this fruity fool, which makes a quick summery dessert or breakfast. Fruit fools are a great way of encouraging children to eat more fresh produce, and since the fruit is puréed rather than cooked, it does not lose any of its precious vitamins.

SERVES 4   **PREPARATION** 10 minutes

2 ripe mangoes

300ml/10¹/₂fl oz/1¹/₄ cups low-fat fromage frais

2 passion fruit, halved

1   Using a vegetable peeler, remove the skin from the mangoes, then slice the flesh away from the large central stone. Put the mango flesh in a blender and process until puréed.

2   Pour the yogurt into the blender and blend again until combined, then spoon into four glasses.

3   Using a teaspoon, scoop the passion fruit out of its skin, place a spoonful on top of each serving and serve.

Storage
Can be covered and stored in the refrigerator for up to 12 hours.

Health Benefits

Passion fruit are a good source of immune system-boosting beta carotene and vitamin C, and the seeds are rich in dietary fibre. The egg-shaped fruit are also said to have soporific properties.

Food Facts per Portion

Calories 83kcal • Total Carbs 13.5g • total sugar 13.5g • added sugar 0g

Variation

Berries make great fools and would be a perfect substitute for the mango and passion fruit. Try a combination of strawberries and raspberries, and add a scattering of fresh blueberries or black-berries before serving.

Mashed banana or an apple or pear purée also taste delicious stirred into natural yogurt. Top with some chopped fresh fruit for a variation in texture.

Prune & Chestnut Fool

Ⓥ Ⓓ Ⓞ ⊜ ⊛

Prunes and chestnuts are a classic combination and make the perfect foundation for a deliciously luxurious and creamy fool.

SERVES 4

PREPARATION 10 minutes, plus chilling   **COOKING** 6 minutes

100g/3½oz/½ cup prunes, chopped

200g/7oz chestnut purée

200ml/7fl oz/generous ¾ cup thick low-fat natural bio yogurt

1 tsp vanilla extract

4 tsp fructose

2 egg whites

1 Put the prunes in a small saucepan with 170ml/5½fl oz/ ⅔ cup water and bring to the boil, then reduce the heat and simmer, covered, for 5 minutes until very soft. Mash the prunes with the back of a fork in the pan until smooth, then leave to cool.

2 Blend the chestnut purée, yogurt, vanilla extract and fructose in a blender until combined, then transfer to a mixing bowl.

3 Whisk the egg whites in a grease-free bowl until they form stiff peaks. Using a metal spoon, stir a spoonful of the whites into the chestnut mixture to slacken it, then fold in the remaining egg whites until they are well combined.

4 Gently stir in the prune purée to give a swirled effect, then spoon into four glasses and serve.

Storage

Can be stored in the refrigerator for up to 3 days.

Health Benefits

Prunes are well known for their ability to prevent constipation thanks to their high fibre content. Chestnuts contain less fat than other nuts, and it is mostly the unsaturated type. They are also the only nut that provides vitamin C.

Food Facts per Portion

Calories 138kcal • Total Carbs 26.2g • total sugar 17.7g • added sugar 4.8g

Chocolate-orange Mousse

Ⓥ Ⓞ Ⓣ

Chocolate and orange are perfect partners. This is a rich chocolate mousse, so a small serving as an occasional treat will satisfy any cravings for something sweet.

SERVES 6

PREPARATION 15 minutes, plus chilling   **COOKING** 5 minutes

200g/7oz plain chocolate (70% cocoa solids), broken into squares

juice of 2 oranges and 1–2 tsp finely grated zest

4 eggs, separated

1   Melt the chocolate in a heatproof bowl placed over a saucepan of gently simmering water, making sure the bottom of the bowl does not touch the water. Leave to cool, then stir in the orange juice and the egg yolks.

2   Whisk the egg whites in a grease-free bowl until they form stiff peaks. Using a metal spoon, stir a spoonful of the whites into the chocolate mixture to slacken it, then fold in the remaining egg whites until they are well combined.

3   Spoon into six small glasses, then chill for about 1 hour until set. Decorate with the strips of orange zest before serving.

Storage

Can be covered and stored in the refrigerator for up to 3 days.

Health Benefits

If eaten in moderation, chocolate is good for us, and the darker the better. Rich in flavonoids, which act as antioxidants, a small amount of dark chocolate eaten every day can benefit the heart, reduce blood pressure and lower LDL cholesterol levels. It also stimulates endorphin production, making you feel good.

Food Facts per Portion

Calories 189kcal • Total Carbs 21.6g • total sugar 21.4g • added sugar 20.6g

Baked Figs with Vanilla Yogurt & Almonds

Fresh figs are bursting with nutrients and are delicious baked in a rich, orangey syrup. Accompanying them with a good dollop of vanilla yogurt and a sprinkling of toasted almonds creates a delicious dessert.

SERVES 4   **PREPARATION** 15 minutes   **COOKING** 15 minutes

8 fresh, not too ripe, figs

juice of 2 oranges and finely grated zest of 1 orange

few drops orange flower water (optional)

1 tbsp plus 2 tsp agave syrup

2 heaped tbsp flaked almonds

185ml/6fl oz/³/₄ cup 2% fat Greek yogurt

¹/₂ tsp vanilla extract

1   Preheat the oven to 180°C/350°F/Gas 4. Stand the figs upright and cut each one into quarters, but do not cut right through to the base. Place the figs in an ovenproof dish, making sure they stand upright.

2   Mix together the orange juice, orange flower water, if using, and 1 tablepoon of the agave syrup and spoon it over the figs. Scatter the orange zest over the top. Bake in the preheated oven for 15 minutes until soft.

3 Meanwhile, put the flaked almonds in a dry frying pan and toast them for about 3 minutes or until light golden. Mix together the yogurt, vanilla extract and remaining agave syrup in a bowl.

4 Remove the figs from the oven and divide among four bowls, then spoon any juices over the top. Sprinkle with the toasted almonds and add spoonfuls of the vanilla yogurt, then serve.

Storage

The vanilla yogurt can be stored in an airtight container in the refrigerator for up to 3 days.

Health Benefits

Figs are a well-known laxative, which is due to their high fibre content. Fibre also plays a beneficial part in protecting the heart and in weight control. The fruit is also rich in potassium, a mineral that helps to control blood pressure, and calcium, which is vital for protecting bone density. In fact, these minerals work in tandem to protect and strengthen the bones and teeth.

Food Facts per Portion

Calories 42kcal • Total Carbs 9.6g • total sugar 9.6g • added sugar 2.4g

Pineapple Sticks with Chocolate Fondue

Ⓥ Ø ⊜ ⊛

These pineapple kebabs taste great barbecued, which gives them a caramelized flavour, but you could also char-grill or grill them. Other types of fresh fruit, including mango, plums and peaches, also taste delicious cooked in this way.

SERVES 4 **PREPARATION** 15 minutes **COOKING** 5–8 minutes

1 ripe pineapple, about 500g/1lb 2oz

1 tsp ground ginger

juice of 1 lemon

Chocolate fondue:

2 tbsp fresh orange juice (not from concentrate)

2 heaped tbsp hazelnut chocolate spread

2 heaped tbsp fat-free fromage frais

2 tbsp semi-skimmed milk

1 Slice the pineapple into 2cm/¾in-thick slices, then cut away the skin and any 'eyes". Slice each pineapple round into quarters, remove the core, then cut the quarters into 2 or 3 chunks, depending on their size.

2 Mix together the ground ginger and lemon juice in a shallow dish, add the pineapple chunks and turn them until coated in the mixture. Thread the chunks lengthways onto skewers – about 5 pieces per skewer – to make 8 kebabs. (If using

wooden skewers, soak them in water for 30 minutes to prevent them burning.)

3 Barbecue the kebabs for about 5–8 minutes, turning once. Alternatively, char-grill them or cook under a high grill until slightly caramelized.

4 Meanwhile, mix together the chocolate dip ingredients in a bowl until combined and serve with the pineapple sticks.

Storage

The pineapple sticks can be stored in an airtight container in the refrigerator for up to 1 day, then served cold. The chocolate dip can be covered and stored in the refrigerator for up to 3 days.

Health Benefits

Pineapple contains an enzyme called bromelain, which aids digestion and has anti-inflammatory properties. The fruit is an excellent source of vitamin C, vitamins B1 and B6 as well as manganese, which is essential for energy production.

Food Facts per

Calories 137kcal • Total Carbs 21.7g • total sugar 21.1g • added sugar 7g

Plum Brulées

Crème brulée is notoriously high in fat, but this low-fat version is equally delicious. It is topped with a fine sprinkling of brown sugar to give the classic caramelized top, but you could use fructose or agave syrup instead. Spray a mist of water over the brulées before grilling to encourage the caramelization of the sugar.

SERVES 4   **PREPARATION** 15 minutes   **COOKING** 10–12 minutes

---

6 ripe dark red plums, such as mirabelle, pitted and chopped

250ml/9fl oz/1 cup 2% fat Greek yogurt

¹/₂ tsp vanilla extract

2–4 tsp soft light brown sugar

1 Put the plums in a saucepan with 2 tablespoons water and bring to the boil, then reduce the heat and simmer, half-covered, for 5 minutes until softened.

2 Mash the plums with the back of a fork in the pan until the fruit is mushy. Divide the plums into four ramekins, then leave the fruit to cool.

3 Preheat the grill to high. Mix together the Greek yogurt and vanilla extract, then spoon the mixture on top of the plums, dividing it equally between each ramekin. Sprinkle ¹/₂–1 tsp sugar, depending on taste, over the top.

4 Place the brulées in a grill pan and cook under the preheated grill for 3–5 minutes until golden and caramelized – keeping an eye on them as the sugar can burn easily. Leave to cool for 5 minutes or completely before serving.

Storage

Can be covered and stored in the refrigerator for up to 1 day. Alternatively, cover the brulées before sprinkling and grilling them, and store for up to 2 days in the refrigerator.

Health Benefits

Vitamin C is found in useful amounts in plums, which, along with assisting in the absorption of iron, is needed by the body to make healthy tissue, support the immune system and protect against damage caused by harmful free radicals.

Food Facts per Portion

Calories 76kcal • Total Carbs 10.8g • total sugar 8.6g • added sugar 6.2g

Peach & Ginger Compote

It is best to use just-ripe or even slightly under-ripe fruit when poaching: too soft, and the fruit will turn to mush when cooked. This dessert is simplicity itself and the fresh ginger imparts a wonderful warmth. Serve the compote with a spoonful of low-fat fromage frais.

SERVES 4   **PREPARATION** 10 minutes   **COOKING** 17–22 minutes

4 peaches, halved and stoned

1 tbsp fruit syrup or agave syrup

4cm/1½in piece fresh root ginger, peeled and sliced into rounds

1 vanilla pod, split in half

1   Put the peaches in a medium saucepan and pour over 250ml/9fl oz/1 cup water. Add the fruit syrup, ginger and vanilla pod and stir together.

2   Bring to the boil, then reduce the heat and simmer, half-covered, for 15–20 minutes, occasionally spooning the cooking liquid over the peaches, until the fruit is tender and the liquid has reduced and become slightly syrupy.

3   Leave the peaches to cool in the syrup and remove the ginger and vanilla pod before serving.

Storage

Can be stored in an airtight container in the refrigerator for up to 5 days.

Health Benefits

Fresh ginger, with its warming, slightly peppery flavour, is best known for its anti-nausea benefits. It has also been shown to be effective in treating joint pain, gastrointestinal disorders and menstrual cramps. It is reputed to have aphrodisiac qualities.

Food Facts per Portion

Calories 72kcal • Total Carbs 15.6g • total sugar 15.6g • added sugar 2.7g

Poached Cardamom Pears

These fragrant pears can be served as a delicious dessert or as an unusual and refreshing accompaniment to savoury platters of cold meat or cheese.

SERVES 4 **PREPARATION** 10 minutes **COOKING** 40–50 minutes

4 slightly under-ripe pears

300ml/10½fl oz/1¼ cups fresh orange juice (not from concentrate)

200ml/7fl oz/generous ¾ cup red wine

6 green cardamom pods, split

1 cinnamon stick

4 cloves

1 Using a vegetable peeler, remove the skin from the pears, retaining the stem. Put the pears in a deep sauté pan and pour over the orange juice, 100ml/3½fl oz/scant ½ cup water and the red wine.

2 Add the cardamom pods, cinnamon stick and cloves to the pan and bring to the boil, then reduce the heat and simmer, half-covered, for 35–45 minutes or until the fruit is tender and the liquid has become slightly syrupy, occasionally spooning the cooking liquor over the pears.

3 Leave the pears to cool slightly in the syrup, then serve one pear per person with a little of the syrup spooned over.

Storage

Can be stored in an airtight container in the refrigerator for up to 5 days.

Health Benefits

Pears are one of the least allergenic of foods, which is why they often form part of allergy diets. Rich in pectin and soluble fibre, pears are said to be valuable in reducing harmful levels of LDL cholesterol in the body. They are also said to be good for the complexion and glossy hair if eaten on a regular basis.

Food Facts per Portion

Calories 121kcal • Total Carbs 21.6g • total sugar 21.6g • added sugar 0g

Black Forest Strudel

The star anise and cinnamon give a wonderful aroma and depth of flavour to this fruit strudel, which is packed with blackberries, blackcurrants, blueberries and apples. For convenience (and economy), use the bags of mixed frozen fruits that can be found in most large supermarkets.

SERVES 6   **PREPARATION** 15 minutes   **COOKING** 35–40 minutes

---

25g/1oz/2 tbsp unsalted butter or polyunsaturated spread, melted, plus extra for greasing

400g/14oz/2¼ cups frozen mixed black forest fruits, defrosted and drained

1 apple, cored and finely diced

1 star anise

1 heaped tsp cinnamon

2 tsp cornflour

9 sheets filo pastry, 30 x 18cm/12 x 7in

2 tbsp xylitol or fructose

½ tsp icing sugar/confectioner's sugar, for dusting (optional)

1 Preheat the oven to 190°C/375°F/Gas 5. Lightly grease a baking tray. Put the fruit in a saucepan with the star anise and cinnamon. Stir and cook over a low heat for 3 minutes. Mix the cornflour with 1 tablespoon warm water and add to the pan. Cook, stirring occasionally, for another 3 minutes, then leave to cool.

2   Place a sheet of filo lengthways on the tray and brush lightly with some melted butter. Place a second sheet crossways over the first, so half of it overlaps, and another sheet next to it to make a 36 x 30cm/14 x 12in rectangle. Brush with more butter, then repeat this process twice more with the other 6 sheets.

3   Remove the star anise from the fruit, then spoon the mixture down the centre of the pastry, following the line of the first filo sheet, leaving a 2cm/¾in border. Sprinkle the xylitol over the fruit. Carefully fold the filo over the fruit, tuck in the ends and then gently roll the parcel over so the seam is underneath.

4   Brush the top with the remaining butter and bake in the preheated oven for 30–35 minutes until golden and crisp. Remove from the oven and dust with icing sugar/confectioner's sugar before serving, if using. Serve, cut into slices.

Storage
Can be stored in an airtight container in the refrigerator for up to 2 days. Reheat to crisp up the pastry.

Health Benefits
Blackberries, blackcurrants and blueberries are a potent source of beneficial phytochemicals, anthocyanins and antioxidants.

Food Facts per Portion
Calories 117kcal • Total Carbs 13.3g • total sugar 9.3g • added sugar 4.6g

Raspberry Cream Roulade

Ⓥ Ⓞ Ⓖ Ⓖ Ⓐ Ⓢ

A real treat of a pudding – this light 'meringue' roulade is filled with a rich and creamy vanilla yogurt and raspberries.

SERVES 8   **PREPARATION** 15 minutes   **COOKING** 20–25 minutes

unsalted butter or polyunsaturated spread, for greasing

4 large/extra-large egg whites

100g/3½oz/½ cup xylitol

40g/1½oz/⅓ cup self-raising flour

pinch of salt

Filling:

125g/4½oz/¾ cup raspberries, hulled

250ml/9fl oz/1 cup 2% fat Greek yogurt

1 tsp vanilla extract

2 tsp xylitol

1   Preheat the oven to 160°C/315°F/Gas 3. Line the base of a 20 x 30cm/8 x 12in Swiss/jelly roll tin with parchment paper, then lightly grease the sides of the tin and the paper.

2   Whisk the egg whites in a large, grease-free bowl until they form stiff peaks. Whisk in all but 1 teaspoon of the xylitol, then gradually sift in the flour and salt, then fold them in. Spoon the mixture into the prepared tin and spread gently into an even layer.

3   Bake in the preheated oven for 20–25 minutes until golden and beginning to come away from the sides of the tin. Remove from the oven and leave to cool for a few minutes, then cover with a just-damp tea towel to prevent cracking when it is rolled up.

4   When the sponge has cooled, remove the tea towel. Lay a sheet of parchment paper on the work surface and sprinkle with the reserved xylitol. Turn the sponge out onto the paper and peel off the lining paper. Roll up the sponge carefully from the long side, wrapping the sugared paper inside, then leave to cool.

5   Put the raspberries in a mixing bowl with the yogurt, vanilla extract and xylitol. Stir gently until the ingredients have combined and the raspberries start to break down. Unroll the sponge, spread the raspberry cream over the top, then roll up and cut into slices.

Storage
Can be covered and stored in the refrigerator for up to 2 days.

Health Benefits
Xylitol is a low-calorie, crystalized sugar substitute, often made from birch or corn. Since it is absorbed more slowly than refined sugar, it does not contribute to swings in blood-sugar levels.

Food Facts per Portion
Calories 84kcal • Total Carbs 18.6g • total sugar 14g • added sugar 13.3g

Baked Egg Custard

This version of a classic dessert uses fructose as a sweetener in place of caster sugar, which means that you need only a third of the quantity to achieve the same result. Choose vanilla extract rather than vanilla flavouring for the best flavour.

SERVES 4   **PREPARATION** 10 minutes   **COOKING** 75 minutes

700ml/24fl oz/scant 3 cups semi-skimmed milk

1½ tsp vanilla extract

2 tbsp fructose

3 eggs

freshly grated nutmeg, to decorate

1 Preheat the oven to 180°C/350°F/Gas 4. Put the milk, vanilla extract and fructose in a medium heavy-based saucepan. Heat gently until nearly boiling, stirring occasionally.

2 Beat the eggs in a large mixing bowl, then gradually pour in the milk, stirring with a balloon whisk. Strain the mixture through a fine sieve into a 900ml/1½ pint/3¾ cup ovenproof dish.

3 Grate a generous amount of nutmeg over the custard and bake in the preheated oven for 60–70 minutes until set and light golden on top. Remove from the oven and serve still warm from the oven or leave until cold.

Storage

Can be covered and stored in the refrigerator for up to 3 days.

Health Benefits

Fruit sugar, otherwise known as fructose, looks and tastes similar to refined sugar, but since it is sweeter you need to use less of it. It also has a lower glycaemic index than sugar, which means peaks and troughs in blood-sugar levels are minimized. However, dietary intake of fructose should be kept to moderate amounts (see page 9).

Food Facts per Portion

Calories 160kcal • Total Carbs 13.9g • total sugar 13.6g • added sugar 5.8g

Sweet Soufflé Omelette

It may not be an obvious dessert, but an omelette tastes just as delicious with a sweet filling as a savoury one. You could try stewed plums or berries instead of the apple filling.

SERVES 2   **PREPARATION** 15 minutes   **COOKING** 15 minutes

2 sweet apples, peeled, cored and diced

½ tsp cinnamon

2 large/extra-large eggs, separated

1 tsp xylitol

5g/¼oz/1 tsp unsalted butter or polyunsaturated spread

1   Put the apples in a medium saucepan with 4 tablespoons water and the cinnamon. Bring to the boil, then reduce the heat and simmer, covered, for 8 minutes or until tender. Mash lightly with a fork to make a chunky purée, then set aside.

2   Whisk the egg whites in a grease-free bowl until they form stiff peaks. Whisk the egg yolks separately until they are even in colour and texture, then stir in the xylitol. Carefully fold the egg whites into the egg yolks using a metal spoon.

3   Melt the butter in a large non-stick frying pan and swirl it around to cover the base. Tip the frothy egg mixture into the pan and gently flatten with a spatula (without losing too much air) until it covers the base of the pan. Cook over a medium heat for 2–3 minutes until light golden.

4 Spoon the apple down the centre of the omelette, cook for another minute, then fold it in half to encase the fruit. Slide the omelette on to a serving plate, cut in half crossways and serve.

Storage

The apple purée can be stored in an airtight container in the refrigerator for up to 3 days.

Health Benefits

Cinnamon lends a pleasing warmth to sweet and savoury dishes. It has antibacterial properties and has been found to reduce both blood glucose and unhealthy fat levels if eaten on a regular basis.

Food Facts per Portion

Calories 147kcal • Total Carbs 14.1g • total sugar 14.1g • added sugar 2.5g

Ricotta Cakes with Berry Sauce

Ⓥ Ⓞ ⊜ ⊕

Lightly sweetened with agave syrup, these orange-infused puddings come with a simple berry sauce.

SERVES 4 **PREPARATION** 15 minutes **COOKING** 20 minutes

olive oil, for greasing

280g/10oz/1¼ cups ricotta cheese

2 tbsp agave syrup

finely grated zest of 1 orange

2 large/extra-large egg whites

300g/10½oz/2½ cups mixed fresh or frozen berries, defrosted if frozen

4 tbsp fresh orange juice (not from concentrate)

1 star anise

1 Preheat the oven to 180°C/350°F/Gas 4. Lightly grease four dariole moulds. Using a wooden spoon, beat together the ricotta, agave syrup and orange zest in a mixing bowl.

2 Whisk the egg whites in a grease-free bowl until they form soft peaks. Using a metal spoon, stir a spoonful of the whites into the ricotta mixture to slacken it, then fold in the remaining egg whites until they are well combined. Spoon the mixture into the moulds. Bake in the preheated oven for about 20 minutes or until risen and light golden.

3 Meanwhile, to make the berry sauce, put three-quarters of the fruit in a saucepan with the orange juice and star anise, then heat gently for 3–5 minutes until the berries are soft and juicy. Press the fruit through a sieve to remove the pips and star anise.

4 Remove the moulds from the oven and leave to cool slightly, then carefully turn out the ricotta cakes and place them on plates. Serve warm with the sauce and decorate with the reserved berries.

Storage

The cakes can be stored in an airtight container in the refrigerator for up to 2 days and the fruit sauce for up to 5 days.

Health Benefits

Make use of spices, such as star anise, cinnamon and nutmeg, to add flavour and aroma to sweet and savoury dishes. As well as their antibacterial and digestive benefits, they reduce the need for large quantities of added sugar.

Food Facts per Portion

Calories 154kcal • Total Carbs 11.8g • total sugar 11.6g • added sugar 5.5g

Strawberry Filo Tarts

These pretty little tarts are filled with strawberries and a luxurious – and low-fat – creamy filling. What's more, they look impressive but are surprisingly easy to make for a special dinner party dessert.

SERVES 4   **PREPARATION** 20 minutes   **COOKING** 20 minutes

25g/1oz/4¹/₂ tsp unsalted butter or polyunsaturated spread, melted

4 filo pastry sheets, 30 x 18cm/12 x 7in

Filling:

8 heaped tbsp quark

1 tsp vanilla extract

2 tbsp agave syrup

12 strawberries, halved if large

1   Preheat the oven to 180°C/350°F/Gas 4. Using a little of the melted butter or spread, lightly grease 4 holes in a deep muffin tin. Cut each sheet of filo into three 10cm/4in squares, so you have 12 squares in total. Discard any surplus pastry.

2   Carefully press a square of filo into each hole in the muffin tin and lightly brush with melted butter, then layer 2 more sheets on top, brushing with more butter as you go. Layer each one diagonally so that you end up with baskets each with a 12-point star top.

3 Bake the baskets in the preheated oven for about 20 minutes until golden and crisp, then remove from the oven and leave to cool.

4 To make the filling, beat together the quark, vanilla extract and agave syrup. Spoon the creamy mixture into the filo cups and top with the strawberries. Serve immediately.

Storage

The baked unfilled filo baskets can be stored in an airtight container in the refrigerator for up to 3 days and the cream filling for up to 2 days.

Health Benefits

Strawberries contain a unique combination of antioxidant phenols, including ellagic acid and anthocyanins, to protect us from heart disease, certain cancers and age-related macular degeneration. Strawberries also contain plentiful amounts of fibre, vitamin C, manganese and potassium and have anti-inflammatory and glucose-balancing properties.

Food Facts per Portion

Calories 111kcal • Total Carbs 10g • total sugar 8.8g • added sugar 5.5g

Apple Amaretti Crumbles

Ⓥ Ⓝ Ⓞ Ⓖ ⓦ ⓔ Ⓥ

A cross between a baked stuffed apple and apple crumble, this recipe makes a perfect warming, comforting pudding for a cold winter's day.

SERVES 4   PREPARATION 15 minutes   COOKING 45 minutes

4 sweet apples, halved crossways

juice of 2 oranges and finely grated zest of 1 orange

25g/1oz/2 tbsp unsalted butter or polyunsaturated spread

3 amaretti biscuits, roughly crushed

1 heaped tbsp toasted flaked almonds, to decorate

4 heaped tbsp low-fat fromage frais, to serve

1 Preheat the oven to 200°C/400°F/Gas 6. Use a melon baller or teaspoon to scoop out the core of each apple half. Put the apples in an ovenproof dish.

2 Spoon the orange juice over each apple half. Divide the butter between the fruit, spooning it into the dip in the centre of each apple, then sprinkle the amaretti crumbs and orange zest over the top.

3 Cover the dish with kitchen foil and bake in the preheated oven for 35 minutes, then remove the foil. Spoon any juices over the apples, then bake for another 10 minutes until the apples are tender.

4 Remove from the oven and sprinkle the flaked almonds over
the apples. Serve warm or at room temperature with a
spoonful of fromage frais.

Storage

Can be stored in an airtight container in the refrigerator for up to
3 days.

Health Benefits

Almonds are rich in vitamin E. This antioxidant decreases the risk
of cataracts and coronary heart disease. The heart also benefits
from the nut's monounsaturated fat content, which has been found
to reduce levels of LDL cholesterol.

Food Facts per Portion

Calories 159kcal • Total Carbs 14.5g • total sugar 13g • added sugar 2.4g

Stuffed Pistachio Peaches

In this deliciously moreish, quick pudding, the peaches are stuffed with a creamy, nutritious date and nut filling. Nectarines can be used as an alternative to peaches.

SERVES 4   PREPARATION 10 minutes   COOKING 6–7 minutes

4 heaped tbsp low-fat cream cheese

2 tbsp fresh orange juice (not from concentrate)

$\frac{1}{2}$ tsp vanilla extract

2 dates, finely chopped

4 ripe peaches, halved and pitted

55g/2oz/$\frac{1}{2}$ cup unsalted pistachio nuts or other favourite nuts, roughly chopped

grated nutmeg, to sprinkle

1 Preheat the grill to medium and line the grill pan with foil. Mix together the cream cheese, orange juice, vanilla extract and dates in a small bowl.

2 Spoon the cream cheese mixture into the hollows in the peach halves, then cook for 6–7 minutes under the preheated grill until the cheese mixture starts to turn golden and the fruit softens.

3 Remove from the grill, scatter the pistachio nuts on top and sprinkle with a little nutmeg. Serve straightaway. Alternatively, serve at room temperature, but add the pistachios and nutmeg only when ready to serve.

Health Benefits

Much of the vitamin C content of a peach is found just below the skin, so the fruit is most nutritious when served unpeeled. Peaches are also a good source of the antioxidant beta carotene, which is converted to vitamin A in the body.

Food Facts per Portion

Calories 194kcal • Total Carbs 15.1g • total sugar 14.8g • added sugar 0g

Variation

Instead of the dried dates, why not try chopped fresh figs or sticky, dark unsulphured apricots? Alternatively, leave out the dried fruit altogether and, after grilling, top with a light drizzle of agave syrup, a sprinkling of ground cinnamon and toasted flaked almonds.

Popovers with Cherries

This idea of serving Yorkshire puddings as a dessert is a novel one, but with the cherry topping this is similar to a low-sugar version of the French clafoutis. Serve with a spoonful of low-fat crème fraîche.

SERVES 6

PREPARATION 10 minutes, plus resting   **COOKING** 20 minutes

115g/4oz/1 cup plain/all-purpose flour

½ tsp baking powder

pinch of salt

70ml/2¼fl oz/scant ⅓ cup semi-skimmed milk

1 egg, lightly beaten

2 tsp sunflower oil

Filling:

200g/7oz/heaped 1 cup dark cherries, pitted

4 tsp agave syrup or fruit syrup

freshly grated nutmeg, to decorate

1   Sift the flour, baking powder and salt into a mixing bowl and make a well in the centre. Measure 4 tablespoons water and the milk in a jug, add the egg and whisk until combined. Pour the egg mixture into the bowl, then gradually whisk together to make a thin batter. Pour the mixture into the jug and set aside for 20 minutes.

2   Preheat the oven to 220°C/425°F/Gas 7. Pour a little oil into each cup of a 6-hole deep muffin tin, then put the tin in the preheated oven for 8 minutes until very hot. Carefully remove from the oven and pour the batter into the holes. Return to the oven for 20 minutes until risen and golden.

3   Meanwhile, put the cherries in a saucepan with 100ml/3½fl oz/ scant ½ cup water, cover and cook over a medium-low heat for 5 minutes until softened.

4   Remove the popovers from the oven and serve one per person, topped with the cherries. Drizzle with the agave syrup and grate over a little nutmeg. Serve straightaway.

Health Benefits

With their ability to cleanse the body by removing toxins from the kidneys, cherries are said to benefit those who suffer from gout and arthritis. Cherries also contain iron, potassium and vitamins C and B.

Food Facts per Portion

Calories 114kcal • Total Carbs 20.6g • total sugar 7.1g • added sugar 2.4g

Baked Chocolate Bananas

This must be one of the easiest desserts to make, but its simplicity does not compromise its deliciousness.

SERVES 4　　　**PREPARATION** 10 minutes　　　**COOKING** 18–20 minutes

4 small, ripe – but not too ripe – bananas, unpeeled

50g/2oz plain chocolate (70% cocoa solids), broken into chunks

1　Preheat the oven to 180°C/350°F/Gas 4. Take a small knife and make a slit along the inner curve of each banana, through the skin and into the flesh, then open out the cut slightly.

2　Divide the chocolate between the bananas, pressing it into the slits. Wrap the bananas in foil and place on a baking sheet.

3　Bake the bananas in the preheated oven for 18–20 minutes until the chocolate has melted and the bananas are soft.

4　Remove from the oven and serve the bananas in their foil parcels, scooping out the delicious chocolatey fruit with a spoon.

Health Benefits
Bananas contain potassium, which is essential for normal blood pressure and heart function and helps to reduce the risk of a stroke.

Food Facts per Portion
Calories 111kcal • Total Carbs 19g • total sugar 18g • added sugar 3.4g

CAKES, BAKES & BREADS

This deliciously diverse collection of recipes amply shows that you don't have to go without cakes, cookies and baked puddings when following a low-sugar diet. This doesn't mean that they should form a major part of your diet though, but the philosophy 'moderation is key' is most appropriate here. The occasional slice of Orange & Almond Cake, helping of Apple & Plum Flapjack Pie or square of Chocolate & Brazil Nut Brownie will satisfy any desire for something sweet without you having to overindulge. You'll find low-sugar versions of family favourites too, such as crumble, cheesecake, scones and shortbread; what's more, many are surprisingly lower in fat than their regular counterparts.

When baking, both fresh and dried fruit will help to keep your cakes moist as well as add natural sweetness, while spices such as nutmeg and cinnamon add a wonderful aroma and flavour. Unlike refined sugar and its empty calories, fruit provides valuable fibre as well as a range of vitamins and minerals. Where necessary, but not to excess, fructose, xylitol and agave syrup are also used. These natural sugar alternatives do not cause irregular blood-sugar levels in the same way as refined sugar does, whilst the fibre also helps to curb peak and troughs.

The chapter also includes savoury recipes, including Chickpea Pancakes, as well as the simplest bread in the world to make – soda bread made with the wonderfully nutty-flavoured spelt flour.

Coconut, Banana & Chocolate Cookies

Free from added sugar, these cookies get their sweetness from the bananas, coconut and raw cacao nibs.

MAKES 20 **PREPARATION** 15 minutes **COOKING** 15–20 minutes

polyunsaturated spread, for greasing

100g/3½oz/1 cup rolled oats

50g/1¾oz/scant ⅓ cup ground almonds

100g/3½oz/1 cup desiccated unsweetened coconut

¼ tsp cinnamon

½ tsp baking powder

2 large ripe bananas, peeled

½ tsp vanilla extract

5 tbsp organic virgin coconut oil, warmed until liquid (or olive oil)

100g/3½oz/generous ½ cup raw cacao nibs

1 Preheat the oven to 180°C/350°F/Gas 4. Lightly grease two large baking sheets.

2 In a large mixing bowl, mix together the oats, ground almonds, desiccated coconut, cinnamon and baking powder.

3 In a second bowl, mash the bananas well, then stir in the vanilla extract and warmed coconut oil. Add the wet ingredients to the dry ingredients and mix well, then fold in the raw cacao nibs.

4 Place 20 tablespoons of the dough onto the prepared baking sheets, and flatten the tops slightly to make cookies about 4cm/1½in in diameter.

5 Bake in the preheated oven for 15–20 minutes until golden. Remove from the oven and leave to cool for a few minutes, then transfer to a wire rack to cool.

Storage
Can be stored in an airtight container for up to 5 days.

Health Benefits
The numerous health properties of coconut oil can be attributed to the presence of lauric acid, capric acid and caprylic acid, which are antimicrobial, antioxidant, antifungal and antibacterial. There is a whole string of associated benefits, including reduced risk of kidney problems, heart disease, high blood pressure, diabetes and cancer. There are also recorded improvements in the condition of the hair, skin, bone strength, metabolism and digestion. Make sure you use organic virgin oil rather than a blended variety.

Food Facts per Biscuit
Calories 124kcal • Total Carbs 7.9g• total sugar 2.5g • added sugar 0g

Lemon & Ginger Cheesecake

The base of this cheesecake is made from oatcakes, nuts and seeds with a touch of ginger, and the topping is light and lemony.

SERVES 12 **PREPARATION** 25 minutes **COOKING** 45–55 minutes

300g/10½oz/generous 1¼ cups low-fat cream cheese

200g/7oz/scant 1 cup half-fat crème fraîche

2 tsp vanilla extract

3 eggs, separated

2 tbsp cornflour dissolved in 1 tbsp warm water

finely grated zest of 3 unwaxed lemons and juice of 2 lemons

4 tbsp fructose

Base:

60g/2¼oz/4 tbsp unsalted butter or polyunsaturated spread, melted, plus extra for greasing

120g/4½oz rough oatcakes

60g/2¼oz/scant ½ cup mixed nuts, such as cashews, Brazils, walnuts

2 tbsp sunflower seeds

2 tsp ground ginger

2 tbsp fructose

1 Preheat the oven to 160°C/315°F/Gas 3. Lightly grease a 20cm/ 8in springform cake tin. Put the oatcakes in a food processor and process until they form a fine breadcrumb consistency.

2 Pour the crumbs into a mixing bowl. Put the nuts and seeds into the food processor and process until very finely chopped, then add to the bowl with the ground ginger, fructose and melted butter. Stir until combined, then spoon into the prepared tin and press firmly into an even layer to make a firm base.

3 To make the filling, put the cream cheese, crème fraîche, vanilla extract and egg yolks in a bowl and beat together. Add the dissolved cornflour, lemon zest and lemon juice and beat well.

4 Whisk the egg whites in a grease-free bowl until they form stiff peaks, then whisk in the fructose. Using a metal spoon, fold the whites into the cream cheese mixture until they are well combined. Spoon into the cake tin in an even layer.

5 Bake in the preheated oven for 45–55 minutes until the filling has set. Remove from the oven and leave to cool in the tin.

Storage

Can be covered and stored in the refrigerator for up to 5 days.

Health Benefits

Nuts and seeds often get a bad press due to their fat content, but remember that it is the healthier, unsaturated type of fat.

Food Facts per Portion

Calories 250kcal • Total Carbs 17.6g • total sugar 6.7g • added sugar 4.8g

Apple & Plum Flapjack Pie

Ⓥ Ⓐ Ⓑ Ⓒ Ⓓ Ⓔ

Fruit crumble with a twist: this pie has a crisp oaty topping. Sweet apples are used instead of cooking apples, because they need much less added sugar to sweeten them. Make little pies in individual dishes rather than one large pie in a large dish, if you prefer.

SERVES 6   **PREPARATION** 15 minutes   **COOKING** 20–25 minutes

3 sweet apples, quartered, cored, peeled and diced

squeeze of lemon juice

5 dark plums, halved, pitted and diced

2 tsp cinnamon

Topping:

4 tbsp agave syrup

75g/3oz/5 tbsp unsalted butter or polyunsaturated spread

150g/5½oz/1¼ cups whole oats

3 tbsp chopped hazelnuts

2 tbsp sunflower seeds

1   Preheat the oven to 180°C/350°F/Gas 4. Toss the apples in the lemon juice to prevent them browning, then place in a 23cm/9in-diameter ovenproof dish with 2 tablespoons water, the plums and cinnamon and stir well to combine.

2   To make the topping, heat the agave syrup and butter in a medium saucepan until the butter has melted. Remove from the heat and stir in the oats, hazelnuts and sunflower seeds.

3   Sprinkle the oat mixture over the top of the fruit. Bake in the preheated oven for 20–25 minutes until golden and beginning to crisp. Remove from the oven and serve warm.

Storage
Can be covered and stored in the refrigerator for up to 3 days.

Health Benefits
Agave syrup is a natural sweetener from the agave cactus in Mexico. The syrup can be used in place of sugar and other sweeteners, and since it is about 25 per cent sweeter, less is needed. Agave syrup is primarily fructose, and so it has a lower GI and GL than many other natural sweeteners. It also provides iron, magnesium, potassium and calcium. However, fructose should be consumed in only moderate amounts (see page 9).

Food Facts per Portion
Calories 320kcal • Total Carbs 32.3g • total sugar 12.1g • added sugar 7.3g

Pear & Plum Oaty Cobbler

This fruity baked pudding has a scone/biscuit topping and is delicious served warm with a spoonful of low-fat fromage frais or crème fraîche.

SERVES 4 **PREPARATION** 15 minutes **COOKING** 25 minutes

2 pears, cored and chopped into bite-sized pieces

4 dark plums, halved, pitted and chopped into bite-sized pieces

1 tsp mixed spice/apple pie spice

1 tsp xylitol

Cobbler topping:

70g/2¹/₂oz/scant ²/₃ cup plain/all-purpose flour

50g/1³/₄oz/7 tbsp plain/all-purpose wholemeal flour

1 tsp baking powder

¹/₂ tsp baking soda

2 tbsp whole oats

1 tbsp xylitol

125ml/4fl oz/¹/₂ cup thick low-fat natural bio yogurt

2 tsp fresh lemon juice

25g/1oz/2 tbsp unsalted butter or polyunsaturated spread, melted

1 Preheat the oven to 200°C/400°F/Gas 6. Mix together the pears, plums, mixed/apple pie spice, xylitol and 2 tablespoons water in a bowl, then divide the mixture into four ramekins.

2 To make the cobbler topping, sift both types of flour (adding any bran left in the sifter), baking powder and baking soda into a bowl. Stir in the oats and xylitol.

3 Mix together the yogurt, lemon juice and melted butter, then stir into the dry ingredients to make a soft, sticky dough. Drop teaspoonfuls of the dough on top of the fruit.

4 Put the ramekins on a baking sheet and bake in the preheated oven for 25 minutes until the scone/biscuit topping has risen and is light golden. Remove from the oven and serve warm.

Storage

Can be covered and stored in the refrigerator for up to 3 days.

Health Benefits

Plums range in colour from pale yellow to dark purple, with the latter tending to be the most sweet and so not requiring additional sweetening. Plums are particularly rich in vitamin C, which assists in the body's absorption of iron.

Food Facts per Portion

Calories 254kcal • Total Carbs 42.5g • total sugar 15.6g • added sugar 5g

Little Lemon Puddings

Ⓥ Ⓞ Ⓓ Ⓔ 🅔 🅢

These intensely lemony, light puddings have a sponge topping and a curd-like sauce at the bottom.

SERVES 4   **PREPARATION** 15 minutes   **COOKING** 18–20 minutes

40g/1^1/$_2$oz/7^1/$_2$ tsp unsalted butter, softened, or polyunsaturated spread, plus extra for greasing

70g/2^1/$_2$oz/scant ^{1}/$_2$ cup fructose

juice and finely grated zest of 2 unwaxed lemons

3 eggs, separated

100ml/3^1/$_2$fl oz/scant ^{1}/$_2$ cup semi-skimmed milk

40g/1^1/$_2$oz/scant ^{1}/$_2$ cup self-raising flour, sifted

1 Preheat the oven to 180°C/350°F/Gas 4. Lightly grease six deep ramekins. Put the butter and fructose in a bowl and beat together, using a hand whisk or electric mixer, until pale and smooth.

2 Gradually beat in the lemon juice and zest, after which the mixture will look curdled but this is not a problem. Beat in the egg yolks, one at a time, then add the milk and flour and mix lightly until combined.

3 Whisk the egg whites in a grease-free bowl until they form stiff peaks. Using a metal spoon, stir a spoonful of the whites into the lemon mixture to slacken it, then fold in the remaining egg whites until they are well combined. Spoon the

mixture into the ramekins, then place on a baking tray and pour enough hot water to come halfway up the sides of the ramekins.

4   Bake in the preheated oven for 18–20 minutes or until risen. Remove from the oven and serve warm or cold.

Storage

Can be covered and stored in the refrigerator for up to 3 days.

Health Benefits

Lemons are known for their generous vitamin C content. This antioxidant defends body cells against harmful free radicals, reducing the risk of heart disease and strokes. Whilst vitamin C does not prevent colds, it is agreed that it can reduce the severity and length of one.

Food Facts per Portion

Calories 242kcal • Total Carbs 26.1g • total sugar 18.1g • added sugar 16.8g

Carrot & Walnut Cake

Ⓥ ◐ Ⓞ ◑ ◌ ◉

Along with adding sweetness to a cake, sugar keeps it moist too: a role here that is partly taken on by the carrots. This is a delicious and simple cake to make.

SERVES 16   **PREPARATION** 20 minutes   **COOKING** 45 minutes

polyunsaturated margarine, for greasing

125g/4^1/2oz/generous 1 cup self-raising wholemeal flour

125g/4^1/2oz/generous 1 cup self-raising flour

2 tsp cinnamon

2 tsp mixed spice/apple pie spice

110g/3^3/4oz/scant ^{1}/2 cup fructose

270g/9^1/2oz (about 2 large) carrots, peeled and grated

50g/1^3/4oz/^{1}/2 cup chopped walnuts

200ml/7fl oz/generous ^{3}/4 cup sunflower oil

4 eggs

1   Preheat the oven to 180°C/350°F/Gas 4. Lightly grease and line the base of a 20cm/8in square cake tin.

2   Sift both types of flour (adding any bran left in the sieve), cinnamon and mixed spice/apple pie spice into a mixing bowl. Using a wooden spoon, stir in the fructose and carrots until combined. Next, stir in the walnuts.

3 Beat together the oil and eggs in a measuring jug, then pour the mixture into the mixing bowl and stir gently until all the ingredients are mixed together.

4 Pour the cake mixture into the prepared tin and smooth the top with the back of a spoon. Bake in the preheated oven for 45 minutes until risen and golden. Remove the cake from the oven and leave in the tin for 10 minutes, then turn it out to cool on a wire rack. Serve cut into squares.

Storage

Can be stored in an airtight tin or wrapped in foil for up to 5 days.

Health Benefits

The antioxidant beta carotene (converted into vitamin A in the body) is found in plentiful amounts in carrots. A recent study also showed that carrots can help to protect against food poisoning.

Food Facts per Portion

Calories 236kcal • Total Carbs 18.2g • total sugar 7.9g • added sugar 6.4g

204 QUICK & EASY LOW-SUGAR RECIPES

Banana Bread

Ⓥ ◐ ◑ ◒ ◓ ◔

Make sure you use ripe bananas, as they will give a delicious moistness and flavour to this tea loaf.

SERVES 12   **PREPARATION** 20 minutes   **COOKING** 1 hour

100g/3½oz/heaped ⅓ cup butter or polyunsaturated spread, plus extra for greasing

100g/3½oz/scant 1 cup plain/all-purpose flour

125g/4½oz/generous 1 cup plain/all-purpose wholemeal flour

1 tsp mixed spice/apple pie spice

1 heaped tsp baking powder

70g/2½oz/scant ½ cup unsulphured ready-to-eat dried apricots, roughly chopped

2 large/extra-large eggs, lightly beaten

2 tbsp agave syrup or fruit syrup

finely grated zest of 2 oranges and juice of 1 orange

4 ripe bananas, mashed

1   Preheat the oven to 180°C/350°F/Gas 4. Lightly grease and line the base of a 28 x 11 x 8cm/11¼ x 4¼ x 3¼in deep loaf tin. Melt the butter in a small saucepan and leave to cool.

2   Sift both types of flour (adding any bran left in the sieve), mixed spice/apple pie spice and baking powder into a mixing bowl, then stir in the apricots.

3 Mix together the melted butter, eggs, agave syrup, orange
juice and zest, then stir in the mashed bananas. Using a
wooden spoon, gently stir the banana mixture into the dry
ingredients – but don't over-mix or the cake will be heavy.

4 Pour the cake mixture into the prepared tin and level the top,
then bake in the preheated oven for 1 hour or until a skewer
inserted into the centre of the cake comes out clean. Remove
from the oven and leave in the tin for 10 minutes, then turn
out onto a wire rack to cool.

Storage

Can be stored in an airtight container or wrapped in foil for up to
5 days.

Health Benefits

Bananas, when ripe, are a good way of adding natural sweetness to
cakes and biscuits. What's more, the fruit also provides beneficial
amounts of dietary fibre and minerals, especially potassium, which
is important for the cells, nerves and muscles They are also rich in
tryptophan, which is known to lift the spirits and aid restful sleep.

Food Facts per Portion

Calories 186kcal • Total Carbs 24.1g • total sugar 11.3g • added sugar 2.4g

Spiced Apple Cake

Apples lend a natural sweetness and moist texture to this simple cake, which is perfect as a teatime treat. The cake could also be served as a dessert with a dollop of fromage frais and fresh berries.

SERVES 12   **PREPARATION** 15 minutes   **COOKING** 40 minutes

120g/4¼oz/1 cup butter or polyunsaturated spread, melted, plus extra for greasing

115g/4oz/1 cup self-raising wholemeal flour

115g/4oz/1 cup self-raising flour

1 tbsp mixed spice/apple pie spice

1 tsp cinnamon

80g/2¾oz/scant ½ cup fructose

2 eggs, lightly beaten

2 tbsp semi-skimmed milk

3 apples (about 300g/10½oz), cored and grated

1 Preheat the oven to 180°C/350°F/Gas 4. Lightly grease and line the base of a 20cm/8in springform cake tin.

2 Sift both types of flour (adding any bran left in the sieve), mixed spice/apple pie spice and cinnamon into a mixing bowl, then add the fructose. Stir the melted butter, eggs and milk into the dry ingredients. Next, gently stir in the apples.

3   Tip the cake mixture into the prepared tin and level the top.
    Bake in the preheated oven for 35–40 minutes until risen and
    golden. Remove from the oven and leave to cool in the tin for
    10 minutes, then transfer to a wire rack to cool.

Storage

Can be stored in an airtight container or wrapped in foil for up
to 5 days.

Health Benefits

Apples contain the trace mineral boron, which has been found to
play an important role in maintaining mental alertness and
concentration. Research also shows that boron may relieve the
symptoms of arthritis, osteoporosis and candida.

Food Facts per Portion

Calories 182kcal • Total Carbs 21.1g • total sugar 8.6g • added sugar 6.2g

Orange & Almond Cake

Ⓥ ⍟ Ⓞ ⍟

Wheat-, gluten- and dairy-free, this fragrant orange cake is reminiscent of the traditional Spanish Santiago cake.

SERVES 12   **PREPARATION** 20 minutes   **COOKING** 45–50 minutes

polyunsaturated spread, for greasing

6 eggs, separated

100g/3½oz/½ cup fructose

finely grated zest of 3 oranges

150g/5oz/generous 1 cup ground almonds

Topping:

juice of 2 oranges

1 tbsp honey

1   Preheat the oven to 180°C/350°F/Gas 4. Lightly grease and line a 20cm/8in springform cake tin. Beat together the egg yolks, fructose, orange zest and ground almonds in a mixing bowl.

2   Whisk the egg whites in a large grease-free bowl until they form stiff peaks. Using a metal spoon, stir a spoonful of the whites into the almond mixture to slacken it, then fold in the remaining egg whites until they are well combined. Carefully pour the mixture into the prepared cake tin.

3   Bake in the preheated oven for 45–50 minutes until a skewer inserted into middle of the cake comes out clean. Remove from the oven and leave to cool in the tin.

4   To make the topping, put the orange juice and honey in a small saucepan and bring to the boil. Stir once, then simmer undisturbed for 6–8 minutes until reduced, thickened and syrupy. Prick the top of the cake with a fork, pour the syrup over the top and leave to soak in before serving.

Storage
Can be stored in an airtight container or wrapped in foil for up to 5 days.

Health Benefits
Anxiety and stress increase levels of free radicals in the body, depleting energy levels and immunity to disease and illness. Oranges are renowned for their high vitamin C content but they are also rich in phytonutrients, or plant compounds, which help to deplete free radicals and reduce the risk of certain cancers and heart disease.

Food Facts per Portion
Calories 155kcal • Total Carbs 11.6g • total sugar 10.7g • added sugar 10.2g

Apricot & Hazelnut Refrigerator Cake

Ⓥ ⚫ Ⓞ ⚫

This 'cake' beats shop-bought fruit-and-nut chocolate bars hands down. Feel free to use your own favourite fruit and nuts.

SERVES 16   **PREPARATION** 15 minutes   **COOKING** 8 minutes

polyunsaturated spread, for greasing

100g/3½oz/generous ½ cup hazelnuts

85g/3oz/½ cup pecan nuts

150g/5½oz plain chocolate (70% cocoa solids), broken into squares

85g/3oz/½ cup unsweetened dried cherries, roughly chopped

85g/3oz/½ cup unsulphured ready-to-eat dried apricots, chopped

2 egg whites

1 tsp unsweetened cocoa powder, for dusting

1   Lightly grease and line the base of a 20cm/8in square tin. Toast the hazelnuts and pecans in a dry frying pan for 5–6 minutes until lightly toasted, taking care because they can burn easily. Put the hazelnuts in a clean tea towel and rub them to remove their brown papery skins.

2   Melt the chocolate in a heatproof bowl placed over a saucepan of gently simmering water, making sure the bottom of the bowl does not touch the water. Stir once or twice until melted, then carefully remove from the heat. Leave to cool for 5 minutes, then stir in the nuts, cherries and half of the apricots.

3   Whisk the egg whites in a grease-free mixing bowl until they form stiff peaks. Using a metal spoon, stir a spoonful of the whites into the chocolate mixture to slacken it, then fold in the remaining egg whites until they are well combined.

4   Pour the mixture into the prepared tin, scatter over the remaining apricots, then level the top with a palette knife. Refrigerate until solid – about 2 hours – then dust with cocoa powder and cut into 16 squares.

Storage

Can be stored in an airtight container in the refrigerator for up to 5 days.

Health Benefits

There's no getting away from the fact that dried fruit is high in sugar, but it is not full of empty or nutrient-free calories like refined sugar. In fact, dried fruit offers many health benefits, namely dietary fibre and a higher concentration of some vitamins and minerals than its fresh counterpart. Asthmatics should avoid dried fruit that has been preserved using sulphites, as it can exacerbate symptoms.

Food Facts per Portion

Calories 152kcal • Total Carbs 11.6g • total sugar 11.6g • added sugar 5.8g

Double-ginger Oat Cookies

You get a double helping of ginger in these delicious cookies: fresh root ginger and ground ginger both lend a wonderful flavour and aroma.

MAKES 12   **PREPARATION** 15 minutes   **COOKING** 17–20 minutes

100g/3½oz/heaped ⅓ cup unsalted butter or polyunsaturated margarine, plus extra for greasing

2 tbsp agave syrup

2.5cm/1in piece fresh root ginger, peeled and grated

100g/3½oz/scant 1 cup wholemeal spelt flour

1 tsp baking powder

1 tsp ground ginger

70g/2½oz/½ cup whole oats

1 Preheat the oven to 180°C/350°F/Gas 4. Lightly grease two baking sheets.

2 Melt the butter in a small saucepan with the agave syrup and grated ginger, then leave to cool slightly. Sift the flour (adding any bran left in the sieve), baking powder and ground ginger into a mixing bowl and stir in with the oats.

3 Pour the melted butter into the dry ingredients and stir to make a soft, chunky dough. Place heaped tablespoons of the cookie mixture onto the baking sheets and flatten the top of each cookie slightly.

4 Bake in the preheated oven for 15–18 minutes until light golden but still slightly soft. Remove from the oven and leave to cool for 5 minutes, then transfer to a wire rack to cool completely.

Storage

Can be stored in an airtight container for up to 5 days.

Health Benefits

Ginger is great for settling the stomach and relieving nausea. What's more, research indicates that ginger encourages the release of insulin in the body and increases the uptake of glucose in fat cells.

Food Facts per Cookie

Calories 118kcal • Total Carbs 11.1g • total sugar 2.1g • added sugar 1.8g

Walnut Shortbreads

These light, crumbly biscuits contain a minimum amount of sugar, but you would never know it from their delicious taste! They are delicious topped with whipped cream and fresh straw-berries or raspberries for a special dessert

MAKES 15   **PREPARATION** 15 minutes   **COOKING** 15–18 minutes

115g/4oz/scant ¹/₂ cup chilled unsalted butter, diced,
 plus extra for greasing

150g/5¹/₂oz/scant 1¹/₂ cups wholemeal spelt flour,
 plus extra for dusting

30g/1oz/¹/₄ cup oatmeal

1 tsp cinnamon

1 tsp baking powder

¹/₄ tsp salt

2 tbsp fructose

40g/1¹/₂oz/¹/₄ cup walnuts, chopped

1 tbsp milk

1 Preheat the oven to 180°C/350°F/Gas 4. Lightly grease two baking sheets.

2 Sift the flour (adding any bran left in the sieve), oatmeal, cinnamon, baking powder and salt into a mixing bowl and stir in the fructose. Rub in the butter with your fingertips until the mixture resembles fine breadcrumbs.

3 Stir in the walnuts, then the milk, then form the mixture into a soft dough with your hands.

4 Flour a work surface and rolling pin, then roll out the dough until 5mm/¼in thick. Using a 5cm/2in cutter, stamp out 15 biscuits, re-rolling the dough as necessary.

5 Place the biscuits on the baking sheets, then bake in the preheated oven for 15–18 minutes until golden. Remove from the oven and transfer to a wire rack to cool.

Storage

Can be stored in an airtight container for up to 5 days.

Health Benefits

Recent studies show that eating walnuts on a regular basis can reduce the risk of heart disease and lower levels of harmful LDL cholesterol in the body. Walnuts are also a good source of omega 3 fatty acids.

Food Facts per Biscuit

Calories 122kcal · Total Carbs 9.6g · total sugar 2.2g · added sugar 1.9g

Date Muffins

These muffins can be whipped up in a matter of minutes and make use of ground almonds and agave syrup in place of highly refined white flour and sugar.

MAKES 6   **PREPARATION** 15 minutes   **COOKING** 15 minutes

polyunsaturated spread, for greasing

3 tbsp olive oil

2 eggs, lightly beaten

½ tsp vanilla extract

2 tbsp agave syrup or fruit syrup

100g/3½oz/scant 1 cup ground almonds

1 tsp baking powder

55g/2oz/⅓ cup ready-to-eat dried dates, cut into small pieces

1   Preheat the oven to 180°C/350°F/Gas 4. Lightly grease 6 holes of a deep muffin tin. Whisk together the olive oil, eggs, vanilla extract and agave syrup in a mixing bowl.

2   Add the almonds, baking powder and dates and fold in gently without over-mixing, since this will make the muffins heavy.

3   Spoon the mixture into the muffin tin and bake in the preheated oven for 15 minutes until risen and light golden. Remove the muffins from the oven and leave in the tin for 5 minutes before turning out to cool on a wire rack.

Storage

Can be stored in an airtight container for up to 5 days.

Health Benefits

In addition to their cholesterol-lowering properties, almonds have an ability to reduce the risk of heart disease, which has been partly attributed to their high vitamin E content. The ground variety also makes a great alternative to wheat flour in cakes and biscuits.

Food Facts per Muffin

Calories 210kcal • Total Carbs 7.9g • total sugar 7.1g • added sugar 3.6g

Variation

In place of the dates, try using dried cherries or blueberries or chopped dried apricot.

Chocolate & Brazil Nut Brownies

Ⓥ ⊘ ⦿ ⊜ ⬡

These brownies make a wonderful treat with their 'fudgey' texture and nutty chocolate flavour. They're also gluten-free. so are suitable for those people with a wheat allergy or intolerance.

SERVES 16 **PREPARATION** 20 minutes **COOKING** 25–30 minutes

100g/3¹/₂oz/heaped ¹/₃ cup unsalted butter or polyunsaturated spread, plus extra for greasing

150g/5¹/₂oz plain chocolate (70% cocoa solids), broken into squares

1 tsp vanilla extract

100g/3¹/₂oz/scant 1 cup ground almonds

85g/3oz/scant ¹/₂ cup fructose

40g/1¹/₂oz/¹/₄ cup Brazil nuts, roughly chopped

4 eggs, separated

1   Preheat the oven to 180°C/350°C/Gas 4. Grease and line the base of a 20cm/8in square tin. Melt the butter and chocolate in a heatproof bowl placed over a saucepan of gently simmering water, making sure the bottom of the bowl does not touch the water.

2   Remove the bowl from the heat, stir, then leave to cool slightly. Stir in the vanilla extract, ground almonds, fructose and Brazil nuts and mix well until combined. Beat the egg yolks lightly, then stir them into the chocolate mixture.

3 Whisk the egg whites in a grease-free bowl until they form stiff peaks. Using a metal spoon, stir a spoonful of the whites into the chocolate mixture to slacken it, then fold in the remaining egg whites until they are well combined.

4 Spoon the mixture into the prepared tin and bake in the preheated oven for 20–25 minutes until risen and firm on top but still slightly gooey in the centre. Remove from the oven and leave to cool in the tin, then turn out, remove the baking parchment and cut into 16 squares.

Storage
Can be stored in an airtight container for up to 5 days.

Health Benefits
Brazil nuts are particularly rich in the mood-enhancing mineral selenium. A single nut a day will ensure that you are not deficient in this mineral.

Food Facts per Brownie
Calories 188kcal • Total Carbs 11.4g • total sugar 10.9g • added sugar 5.8g

Chocolate & Orange Cake

Ⓥ Ⓞ Ⓙ Ⓔ Ⓐ Ⓢ

Treat yourself to this rich, intensely chocolatey cake. Serve with a good spoonful of low-fat fromage frais.

SERVES 12   **PREPARATION** 15 minutes   **COOKING** 25–30 minutes

50g/1³/₄oz/3 tbsp butter or polyunsaturated spread,
  plus extra for greasing

60g/2¹/₄oz plain chocolate (70% cocoa solids), broken intro squares

3 eggs, separated

4 tbsp fructose

finely grated zest of 2 oranges and juice of 1 orange

70g/2¹/₂oz/scant ²/₃ cup self-raising flour

1 tbsp unsweetened cocoa powder

1 Preheat the oven to 150°C/300°F/Gas 2. Lightly grease and line the base of a 20cm/8in springform cake tin.

2 Melt the butter and chocolate in a heatproof bowl placed over a saucepan of gently simmering water, making sure the bottom of the bowl does not touch the water. Stir very occasionally until the chocolate and butter have melted, then remove from the heat.

3 Whisk the egg yolks with the fructose in a mixing bowl until pale, then stir in the chocolate mixture followed by the orange juice and zest. Sift the flour and cocoa powder into the chocolate mixture and fold in using a wooden spoon.

4 Whisk the eggs whites in a grease-free mixing bowl until they form stiff peaks. Using a metal spoon, stir a spoonful of the whites into the chocolate mixture to slacken it, then fold in the remaining egg whites until they are well combined.

5 Spoon the mixture into the prepared cake tin, then bake in the preheated oven for 20–25 minutes until risen. Remove from the oven and leave in the tin for 10 minutes, then turn out to cool on a wire rack.

Storage
Can be stored in an airtight container for up to 5 days.

HEALTH BENEFIT
Make sure you buy a good-quality dark chocolate, at least 70 per cent cocoa solids, since it should have a lower sugar content than other types of chocolate.

Food Facts per Portion
Calories 116kcal • Total Carbs 12.5g • total sugar 8.1g • added sugar 3.1g

Seeded Oatcakes

Serve these light oatcakes plain or topped with a pure fruit spread, humous, pâté or low-fat cream cheese for a more substantial snack.

MAKES 24   **PREPARATION** 20 minutes   **COOKING** 10 minutes

sunflower oil, for greasing

175g/6oz/1½ cups wholemeal spelt flour, plus extra for dusting

100g/3½oz/scant 1 cup medium oatmeal

2 tsp baking powder

¼ tsp salt

100g/3½oz/heaped ⅓ cup chilled unsalted butter, diced

2 tsp fructose

2 tbsp sunflower seeds

4 tbsp semi-skimmed milk

1 Preheat the oven to 200°C/400°F/Gas 6. Lightly grease two baking sheets. Sift the flour (adding any bran left in the sieve), oatmeal, baking powder and salt into a mixing bowl.

2 Add the butter and rub it into the flour mixture using your fingertips until the mixture resembles breadcrumbs, then stir in the fructose and sunflower seeds. Pour in the milk and mix with a fork, and then your hands, to make a dough.

3   Turn the dough out on to a lightly floured work surface and knead briefly until smooth. Using a floured rolling pin, roll out the dough into a rectangle about 5mm/¼in thick. Trim the edges and cut into about 24 squares, re-rolling any trimmings as necessary.

4   Place the oatcakes on the baking sheets and prick the tops with a fork. Bake in the preheated oven for 10 minutes until light golden, swapping the trays halfway, if necessary. Remove from the oven and transfer to a wire rack to cool.

Storage

Can be stored in an airtight container for up to 5 days.

Health Benefits

Oats and wholemeal flour provide both soluble and insoluble fibre. The former, found in most fruits, oats and pulses, helps to regulate levels of cholesterol and glucose in the body. Insoluble fibre, found in whole grains, fruit and vegetables, keeps the bowels regular.

Food Facts per Oatcake

Calories 82kcal • Total Carbs 8.1g • total sugar 0.7g • added sugar 0g

Chickpea Pancakes

These savoury wheat-free pancakes are made with gram (chickpea flour). Serve them as an accompaniment to curries or topped with a spoonful of chutney or salsa (see page 124).

MAKES 12

PREPARATION 10 minutes, plus standing   **COOKING** 16 minutes

140g/5oz/1¼ cups gram (chickpea flour)

½ tsp salt

¼ tsp baking soda

1 tsp black mustard seeds

1 tsp garam masala

2 tbsp natural low-fat bio yogurt

groundnut oil, for frying

1   Sift the flour, salt and baking soda into a large mixing bowl. Stir in the mustard seeds and garam masala, then make a well in the centre. Using a balloon whisk, gradually mix in 200ml/7fl oz/generous ¾ cup water, followed by the yogurt, to make a smooth batter. Set aside for 15 minutes.

2   Heat enough oil to cover the base of a large, heavy-based frying pan over a medium heat. Spoon 2 tablespoons of the batter per pancake into the pan – you will probably be able to cook 3 or 4 at a time.

3   Cook the pancakes for 2 minutes until light golden, then turn
them over with a palette knife and cook for a further 2 minutes.
Keep warm while you cook the remaining pancakes. Serve
the pancakes straightaway.

Health Benefits

Along with a beneficial amount of fibre, chickpeas/garbanzo beans
provide useful amounts of heart-protecting magnesium and folate.
A deficiency in these nutrients has been linked to increased
incidence of a heart attack.

Food Facts per Pancake

Calories 54kcal • Total Carbs 6.5g • total sugar 0.8g • added sugar 0g

Spelt Soda Bread

If you haven't made bread before, soda bread is the perfect place to start. It's quick to make because it doesn't need rising, but the end result is delicious – especially when still warm.

MAKES 1 loaf   **PREPARATION** 15 minutes   **COOKING** 40 minutes

450g/1lb/4 cups wholemeal spelt flour, plus extra for dusting

1 tsp baking soda

1 tsp salt

275ml/9½fl oz/generous 1 cup buttermilk

2 tbsp natural low-fat bio yogurt

1   Preheat the oven to 200°C/400°F/Gas 6. Dust a large baking sheet with flour.

2   Sift the flour (adding any bran left in the sieve), baking soda and salt into a mixing bowl and make a well in the centre. Pour in the buttermilk and yogurt, then gently mix with outstretched fingers to make a soft, slightly sticky dough.

3   Turn the dough out on to a lightly floured work surface and gently form into a smooth ball – don't over-knead or the bread will be heavy. Press the top of the dough down slightly with the palm of your hand.

4   Cut a deep cross into the dough, and, if you're into Irish folklore, don't forget to prick each quarter so the fairies in the

dough can get out! Sift a little flour over the top and bake in the preheated oven for 35–40 minutes until risen and golden. Remove from the oven and transfer to a wire rack to cool.

Storage

Can be stored in an airtight container or wrapped in foil for up to 5 days.

Health Benefits

Low-fat yogurt is a good source of protein, zinc, B vitamins and bone-building calcium. It also provides beneficial bacteria that can help to maintain a healthy digestive system.

Food Facts per Slice (loaf makes 12)

Calories 128kcal • Total Carbs 23.8g • total sugar 2.3g • added sugar 0g

Menu plans

Wheat & gluten-free 5-day menu

For those people who are allergic to or intolerant of wheat and gluten, this menu is easy-to-follow, balanced and, what's more, low in sugar. It may also be necessary to monitor your intake of carbohydrate foods, especially if diabetic, and this menu will allow you to do this.

Day 1
BREAKFAST: Golden Grapefruit (see page 33)
LUNCH: Chinese Egg & Prawn/Shrimp Rice (see page 82)
DINNER: Chicken with Gazpacho Salsa (see page 124)

Day 2
BREAKFAST: Banana & Peanut Butter Smoothie (see page 32)
LUNCH: Asparagus, Courgette/Zucchini & Chive Omelette (see page 76)
DINNER: Beef & Lentil Curry (see page 128)

Day 3
BREAKFAST: Kedgeree (see page 48)
LUNCH: Warm Salad of Beans, Basil & Feta (see page 66)
DINNER: Marinated Lamb with Chickpea Mash (see page 136)

Day 4
BREAKFAST: Date & Vanilla Breakfast Yogurt (see page 26)
LUNCH: Bacon, Lentil & Pepper Salad (see page 94)
DINNER: Thai Mussels with Noodles (see page 114)

Day 5
BREAKFAST: Cheese & Tomato Soufflés (see page 46)
LUNCH: Turkey & Apple Salad (see page 92)
DINNER: Spice-crusted Salmon with Cucumber Salad (see page 108)

Vegetarian 5-day menu

This menu is designed to provide all the nutrients required when following a low-sugar, vegetarian diet, which is free from meat, poultry and seafood.

Day 1
BREAKFAST: Cottage Cheese Pancakes (see page 54)
LUNCH: Tomato & Lentil Soup (see page 64)
DINNER: Vegetarian Chilli in Tortilla Baskets (see page 104)

Day 2
BREAKFAST: Cinnamon Porridge/Oatmeal with Pears (see page 38)
LUNCH: Asparagus, Courgette/Zucchini & Chive Omelette (see page 76)
DINNER: Masoor Dahl (see page 106)

Day 3
BREAKFAST: Fruity French Toast (see page 28)
LUNCH: Pitta Pizzas (see page 62)
DINNER: Lemon & Spinach Lentils with Egg (see page 102)

Day 4
BREAKFAST: Cheese & Tomato Soufflés (see page 46)
LUNCH: Red Quinoa Tabbouleh (see page 68)
DINNER: Ribolllita (see page 100)

Day 5
BREAKFAST: Date & Vanilla Breakfast Yogurt (see page 26)
LUNCH: Spicy Tofu Cakes with Dipping Sauce (see page 72)
DINNER: Heuvos Rancheros (see page 74)

Vegan 5-day menu

This menu avoids any foods derived from animals, including meat, fish, poultry, eggs, dairy and honey. In some cases, recipes have been adapted to suit a vegan diet; use soya, rice or oat milk, yogurt and cheese if appropriate.

Day 1
BREAKFAST: Vegetable Power Juice (see page 30)
LUNCH: Avocado & Tomato Bruschetta (see page 70)
DINNER: Vegetarian Chilli in Tortilla Baskets (see page 104)
– omit sour cream

Day 2
BREAKFAST: On-the-day Muesli (see page 36) – use soya milk
LUNCH: Red Quinoa Tabbouleh (see page 68) – omit halloumi
DINNER: Masoor Dahl (see page 106)

Day 3
BREAKFAST: Homemade Baked Beans (see page 50)
LUNCH: Spicy Tofu Cakes (see page 72) – omit dip
DINNER: Ribollita (see page 100)

Day 4
BREAKFAST: Golden Grapefruit (see page 33)
LUNCH: Tomato & Lentil Soup (see page 64)
DINNER: Heuvos Rancheros (see page 74) – omit eggs

Day 5
BREAKFAST: Fruit & Nut Breakfast Bars (see page 44)
LUNCH: Warm Salad of Beans, Basil & Feta (see page 66)
– use vegan cheese
DINNER: Pasta Puttanesca (see page 80) – omit anchovies

Nut-free 5-day menu

Allergies to nuts and seeds are becoming increasingly common, and, as the symptoms can be life-threatening, it is essential to take every precaution to avoid contact with nuts, seeds and by-products. Always check food labels.

Day 1
BREAKFAST: Banana Griddle Cakes (see page 42)
LUNCH: Salmon & Onion Frittata (see page 86)
DINNER: Moroccan Chicken Pilaff (see page 120)

Day 2
BREAKFAST: Sardines & Tomato on Toast (see page 56)
– use unseeded bread
LUNCH: Turkey & Apple Salad (see page 92)
DINNER: Lemon & Spinach Lentils with Eggs (see page 102)

Day 3
BREAKFAST: Fruity French Toast (see page 28) – use unseeded bread
LUNCH: Chinese Egg & Prawn/Shrimp Rice (see page 82)
DINNER: Ham & Barley Broth (see page 132)

Day 4
BREAKFAST: Homemade Baked Beans (see page 50)
LUNCH: Chicken Tacos with Lime Guacamole (see page 88)
DINNER: Seafood Hotpot with Rouille (see page 112)

Day 5
BREAKFAST: Kedgeree (see page 48)
LUNCH: Beef & Broccoli Stir-fry (see page 96)
DINNER: Vegetarian Chilli in Tortilla Baskets (see page 104)

Index

Apples
  Apple & Plum Flapjack Pie 196
  Apple Amaretti Crumbles 184
  Spiced Apple Cake 206
  Sweet Soufflé Omelette 178
  Turkey & Apple Salad 92
Apricots
  Apricot & Hazelnut Refrigerator Cake 210
  Apricot & Prune Spread
    Banana Bread 204
  Fruit & Nut Breakfast Bars 44
Asparagus, Courgette/Zucchini & Chive
    Omelette 76
Avocado & Tomato Bruschetta 70

Bacon, Lentil & Pepper Salad 94
Baked Chocolate Bananas 190
Baked Egg Custard 176
Baked Eggs & Spinach 52
Baked Figs with Vanilla Yogurt and Almonds
    162
Bananas
  Baked Chocolate Bananas 190
  Banana & Mango Yogurt Ice 146
  Banana & Peanut Butter Smoothie 32
  Banana Bread 204
  Banana Griddle Cakes 42
  Coconut, Banana & Chocolate Cookies
    192
Beef
  Beef & Broccoli Stir-fry 96
  Beef & Lentil Curry 128
  Spiced Beef Kebabs 130
Black Forest Strudel 172
Blueberry & Almond Bircher Muesli 34

Cakes
  Carrot & Walnut Cake 202
  Chocolate & Orange Cake 220
  Chocolate & Brazil Nut Brownies 218
  Orange & Almond Cake 208
  Spiced Apple Cake 206
Cappuccino Pots 150
Carrot & Walnut Cake 202
Cheese
  Cheese & Tomato Soufflés 46
  Cottage Cheese Pancakes 54
  Lemon & Ginger Cheesecake 194
  Pitta Pizzas 62
  Red Quinoa Tabbouleh 68
  Ricotta Cakes with Berry Sauce 180
  Stuffed Pistachio Peaches 186
  Warm Greek Salad of Beans,
    Basil & Feta 66

Chicken
  Chicken Tacos with Lime Guacamole 88
  Chicken with Gazpacho Salsa 124
  Ginger Chicken Parcels 122
  Moroccan Chicken Pilaf 120
  Vegetable & Chicken Ramen 90
Chickpea Pancakes
Chinese Egg & Prawn/Shrimp Rice 82
Chocolate
  Apricot & Hazelnut Refrigerator Cake
    210
  Baked Chocolate Bananas 190
  Chocolate & Orange Cake 220
  Chocolate & Brazil Nut Brownies 218
  Chocolate-Orange Mousse 160
  Coconut, Banana & Chocolate Cookies
    192
  Pineapple Sticks with Chocolate Fondue
    164
Cinnamon Porridge/Oatmeal with Pears 38
Citrus & Pomegranate Salad with Mint 154
Coconut, Banana & Chocolate Cookies 192
Cottage Cheese Pancakes 54

Dates
  Date & Vanilla Breakfast Yogurt 26
  Date & Vanilla Spread 22
  Date Muffins 216
Double-Ginger Oat Cookies 212

Eggs
  Asparagus, Courgette/Zucchini & Chive
    Omelette 76
  Baked Egg Custard 176
  Baked Eggs & Spinach 52
  Cheese & Tomato Soufflés 46
  Chinese Egg & Prawn/Shrimp Rice 82
  Fruity French Toast 28
  Huevos Rancheros 74
  Kedgeree 48
  Lemon & Spinach Lentils with Egg 102
  Salmon & Onion Frittata 86
  Sweet Soufflé Omelette 178

Figs
  Baked Figs with Vanilla Yogurt &
    Almonds 162
  Fig, Nut & Orange Balls 142
Fish and seafood
  Chinese Egg & Prawn/Shrimp Rice 82
  Kedgeree 48
  Lemon & Prawn/Shrimp Linguine 116
  Lemon Fish with Salsa Verde 110
  Mediterranean Potato Salad 78

Pasta Puttanesca 80
Salmon & Onion Frittata 86
Sardines & Tomato on Toast 56
Seafood Hotpot with Rouille 112
Seared Tuna with Rocket & Tomatoes
  118
Spice-Crusted Salmon with Cucumber
  Salad 108
Spiced Prawns/Shrimp on Chapatti 84
Thai Mussels with Noodles 114
Fruit & Nut Breakfast Bars 44
Fruity French Toast 28

Ginger
  Double-Ginger Oat Cookies 212
  Ginger Chicken Parcels 122
  Lemon & Ginger Cheesecake 194
  Peach & Ginger Compote 168
Golden Grapefruit 33
Grapefruit
  Citrus & Pomegranate Salad with Mint
    154
  Golden Grapefruit 33

Ham & Barley Broth 132
Homemade Baked Beans 50
Huevos Rancheros 74

Indian-Spiced Pulses 60

Kedgeree 48

Lamb
  Marinated Lamb with Chickpea Mash
    136
Lemon
  Lemon & Ginger Cheesecake 194
  Lemon & Prawn/Shrimp Linguine 116
  Lemon & Spinach Lentils with Egg 102
  Lemon Fish with Salsa Verde 110
  Little Lemon Puddings 200
Lentils
  Bacon, Lentil & Pepper Salad 94
  Beef & Lentil Curry 128
  Lemon & Spinach Lentils with Egg 102
Little Lemon Puddings 200

Mango
  Banana & Mango Yogurt Ice 146
  Mango & Passion Fruit Fool 156
Marinated Lamb with Chickpea Mash 136
Masoor Dahl 106
Mediterranean Potato Salad 78
Mint Raita 19

Moroccan Chicken Pilaf 120
Muesli
  Blueberry & Almond Bircher Muesli 34
  On-the-Day Muesli 36

Nuts
  Apricot & Hazelnut Refrigerator Cake 210
  Banana & Peanut Butter Smoothie 32
  Carrot & Walnut Cake 202
  Chocolate & Brazil Nut Brownies 218
  Coconut, Banana & Chocolate Cookies 192
  Fig, Nut & Orange Balls 142
  Fruit & Nut Breakfast Bars 44
  Orange & Almond Cake 208
  Prune & Chestnut Fool 158
  Soy Nuts & Seeds 58
  Stuffed Pistachio Peaches 186
  Three-nut butter 21
  Walnut Shortbreads 214

Oats
  Apple & Plum Flapjack Pie 196
  Blueberry & Almond Bircher Muesli 34
  Cinnamon Porridge/Oatmeal with Pears
    38
  Coconut, Banana & Chocolate Cookies
    192
  Double-ginger Oat Cookies 212
  Fruit & Nut Breakfast Bars 44
  On-the-day Muesli 36
  Plum & Oat Crunch 40
  Seeded Oatcakes 222
On-the-day Muesli 36
Orange
  Chocolate & Orange Cake 220
  Chocolate-orange Mousse 160
  Citrus & Pomegranate Salad with Mint
    154
  Fig, Nut & Orange Balls 142
  Orange & Almond Cake 208
  Orange & Pineapple Granita 148

Pasta
  Lemon & Prawn/Shrimp Linguine 116
  Pasta Puttanesca 80
  Thai Mussels with Noodles 114
  Vegetable & Chicken Ramen 90
Peach
  Peach & Ginger Compote 168
  Stuffed Pistachio Peaches 186
Pears
  Cinnamon Porridge/Oatmeal with Pears
    38
  Pear & Plum Oaty Cobbler 198

Poached Cardamom Pears 170
Pineapple
  Orange & Pineapple Granita 148
  Pineapple Sticks with Chocolate Fondue
    164
Pitta Pizzas 62
Plums
  Apple & Plum Flapjack Pie 196
  Pear & Plum Oaty Cobbler 198
  Plum & Oat Crunch 40
  Plum Brulées 166
Poached Cardamom Pears 170
Polpettine in Tomato Sauce 126
Popovers with Cherries 188
Prune
  Apricot & Prune Spread 23
  Prune & Chestnut Fool 158
Pulses
  Bacon, Lentil & Pepper Salad 94
  Beef & Lentil Curry 128
  Chickpea Pancakes 224
  Homemade Baked Beans 50
  Huevos Rancheros 74
  Indian-spiced Pulses 60
  Lemon & Spinach Lentils with Egg 102
  Marinated Lamb with Chickpea Mash
    136
  Masoor Dahl 106
  Moroccan Chicken Pilaff 120
  Pasta Puttanesca 80
  Ribollito 100
  Seared Tuna with Rocket & Tomatoes
    118
  Spanish Chorizo & Bean Stew 134
  Tomato & Lentil Soup 64
  Vegetarian Chilli in Tortilla Baskets 104
  Warm Greek Salad of Beans, Basil & Feta
    66

Raspberries
  Fruity French Toast 28
  Raspberry Cream Roulade 174
  Raspberry Yogurt Creams 152
Red Quinoa Tabbouleh 68
Ribollita 100
Ricotta Cakes with Berry Sauce 180

Salmon & Onion Frittata 86
Sardines & Tomato on Toast 56
Seafood Hotpot with Rouille 112
Seared Tuna with Rocket & Tomatoes 118
Seeded Oatcakes
Soy Nuts & Seeds 58
Spanish Chorizo & Bean Stew 134
Spelt Soda Bread
Spice-Crusted Salmon with Cucumber
    Salad 108
Spiced Apple Cake 206
Spiced Beef Kebabs 130
Spiced Prawns/Shrimp on Chapatti 84

Spicy Tofu Cakes with Dipping Sauce 72
Spinach
  Baked Eggs & Spinach 52
  Kedgeree 48
  Lemon & Spinach Lentils with Egg 102
Strawberries
  Fruity French Toast 28
  Strawberry Filo Tarts 182
  Strawberry Jam 24
Stuffed Pistachio Peaches 186
Superfood Mix 140
Sweet Popcorn 144
Sweet Soufflé Omelette 178

Thai Mussels with Noodles 114
Three-nut Butter 21
Tomatoes
  Avocado & Tomato Bruschetta 70
  Cheese & Tomato Soufflés 46
  Chicken with Gazpacho Salsa 124
  Coconut, Banana & Chocolate Cookies
    192
  Homemade Baked Beans 50
  Huevos Rancheros 74
  Pasta Puttanesca 80
  Pitta Pizzas 62
  Polpettine in Tomato Sauce 126
  Red Quinoa Tabbouleh 68
  Sardines & Tomato on Toast 56
  Seafood Hotpot with Rouille 112
  Seared Tuna with Rocket & Tomatoes
    118
  Spanish Chorizo & Bean Stew 134
  Tomato & Lentil Soup 64
  Tomato Relish 18
  Vegetarian Chilli in Tortilla Baskets 104
  Warm Greek Salad of Beans, Basil & Feta
    66
Turkey
  Polpettine in Tomato Sauce 126
  Turkey & Apple Salad 92
Tzatziki 20

Vegetable & Chicken Ramen 90
Vegetable Power Juice 30
Vegetarian Chilli in Tortilla Baskets 104

Walnut Shortbreads 214
Warm Greek Salad of Beans, Basil & Feta
    66